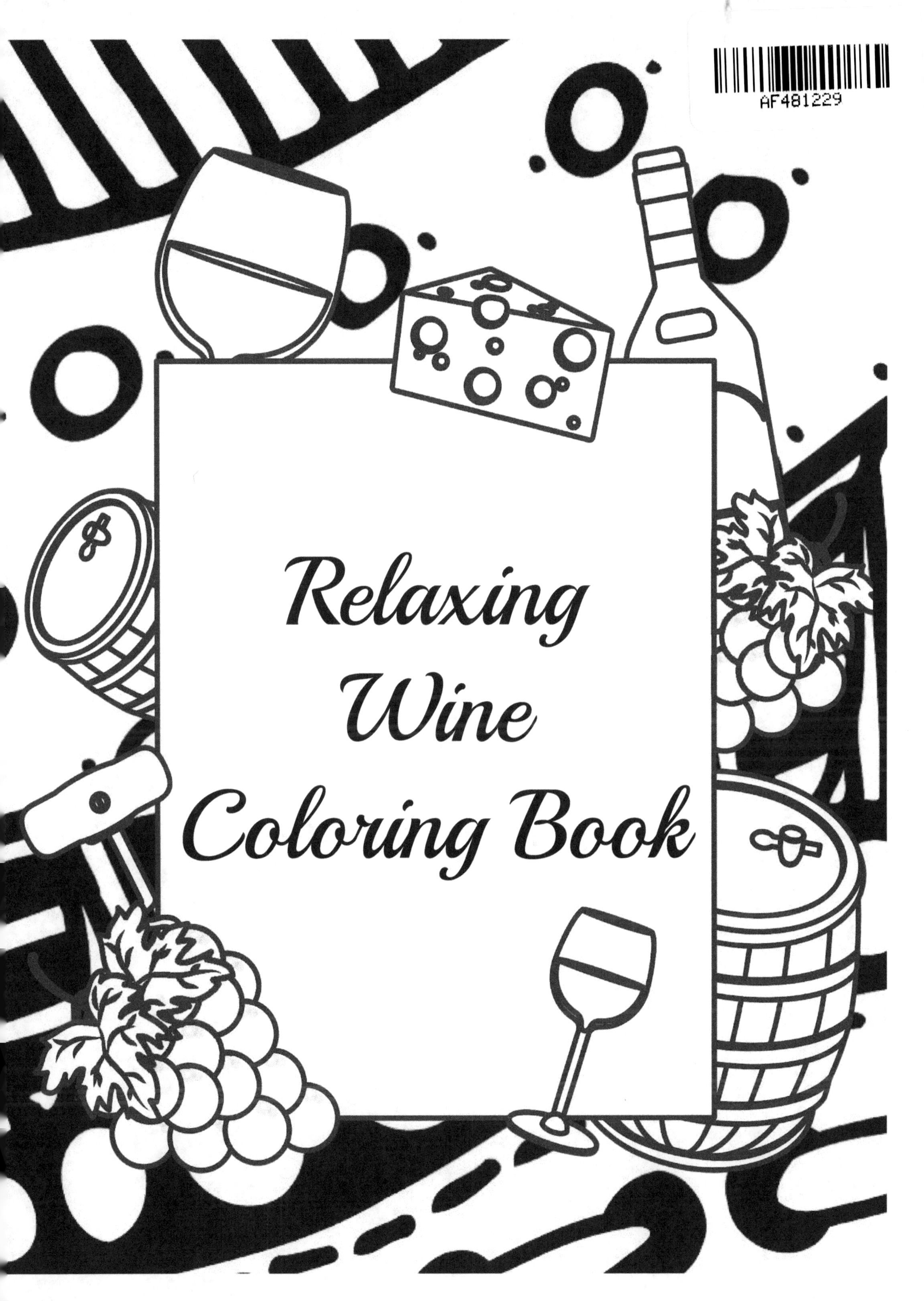

Relaxing
Wine
Coloring Book
AF481229

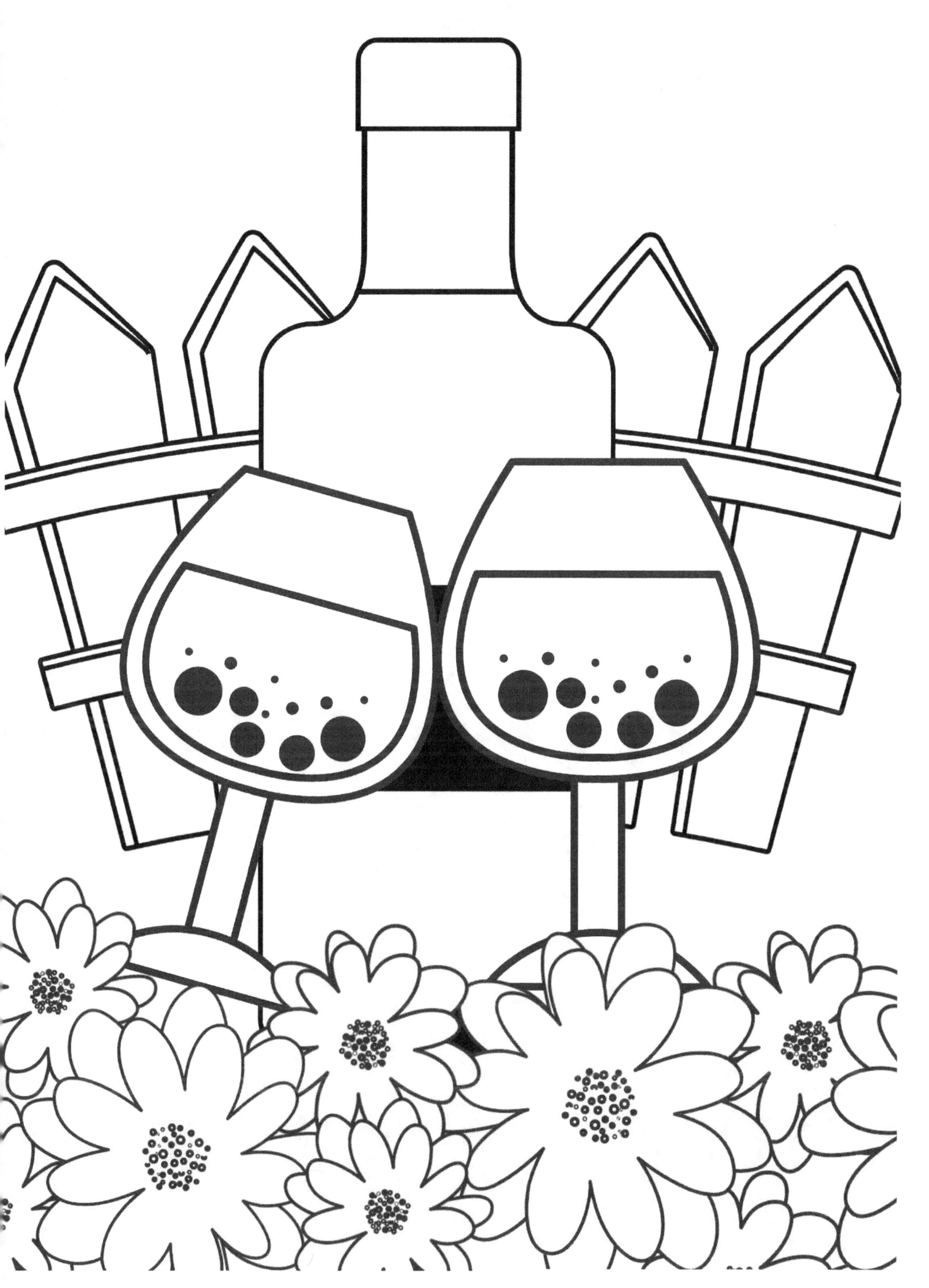

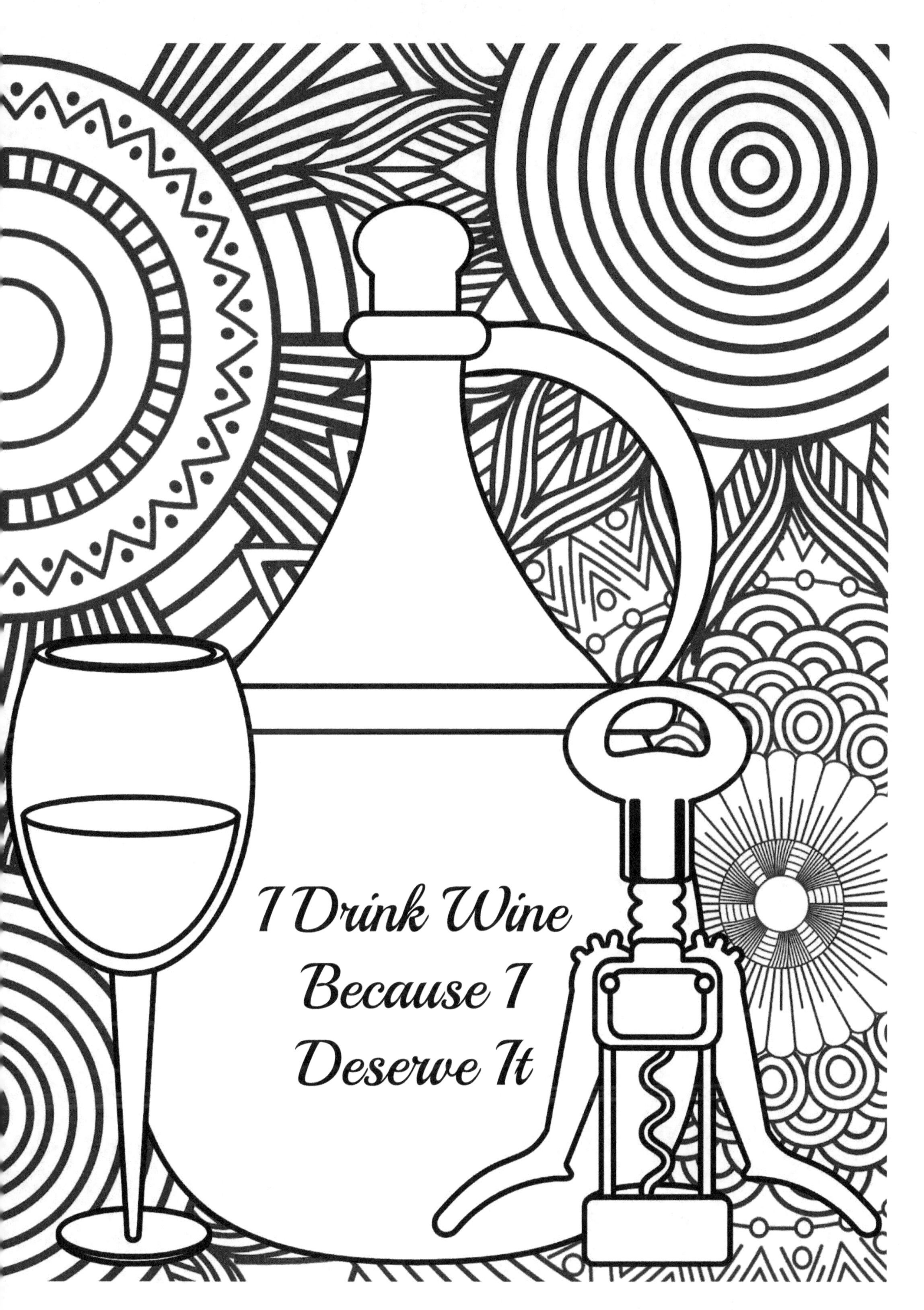

I Drink Wine
Because I
Deserve It

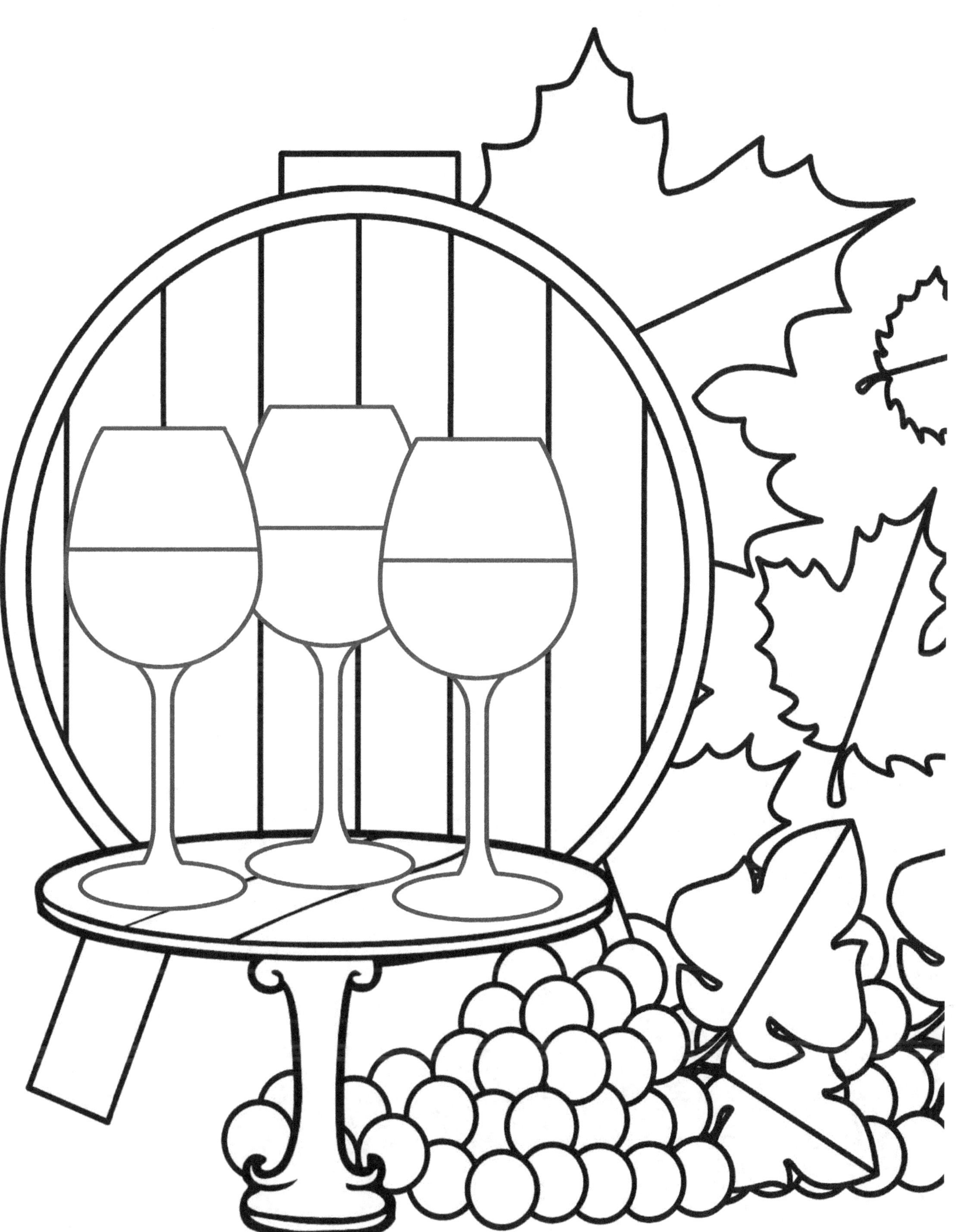

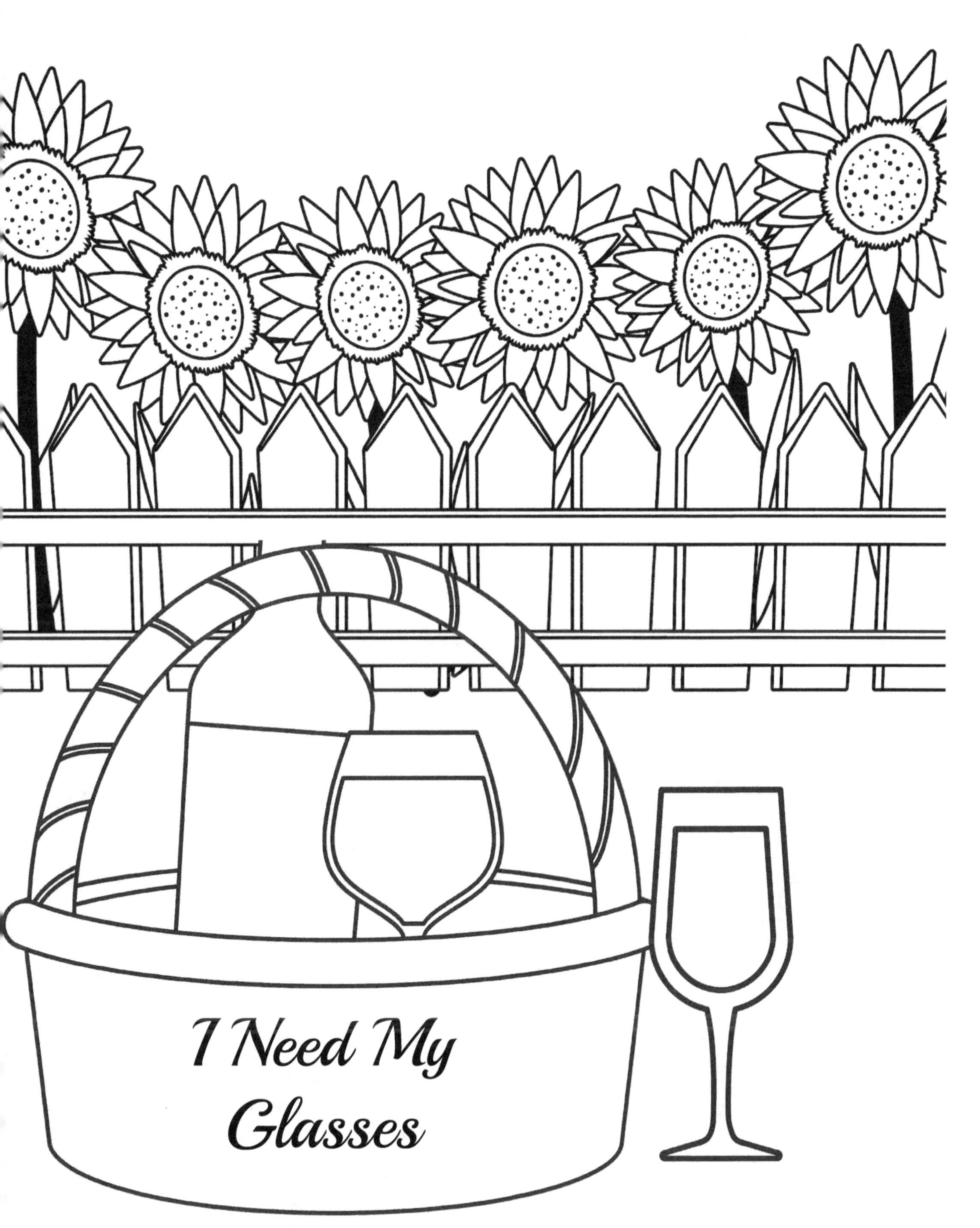

I Need My
Glasses

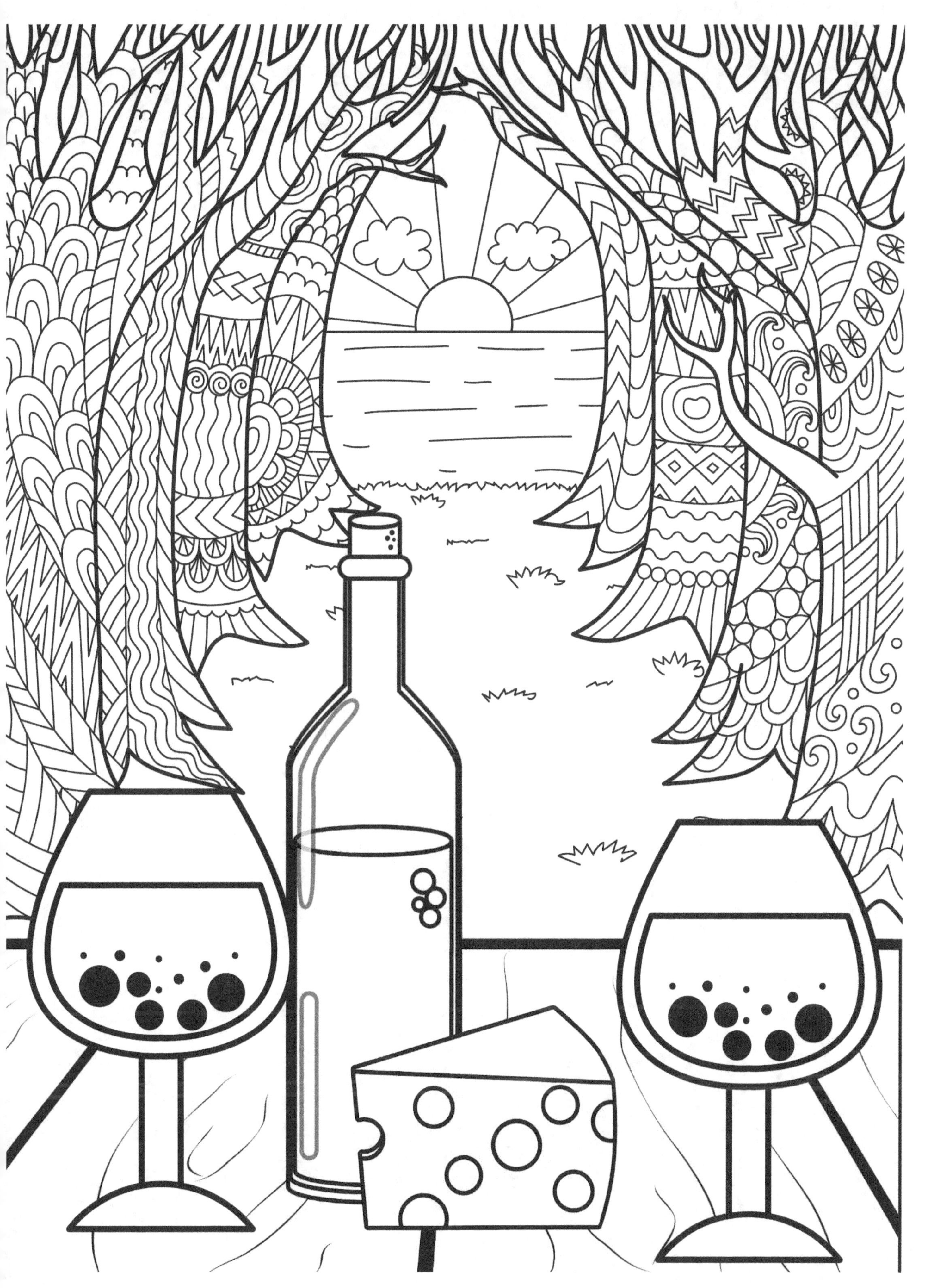

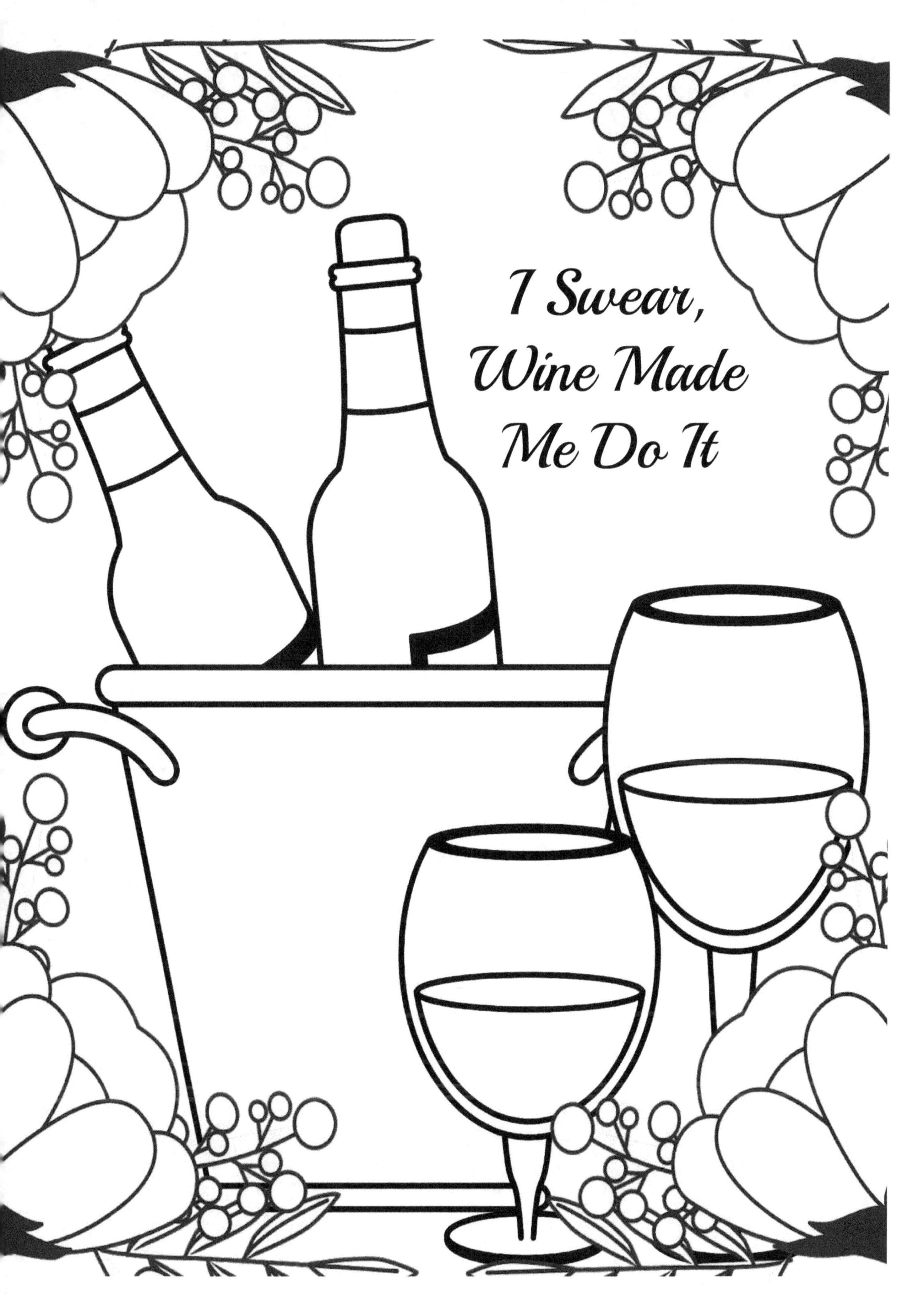

I Swear,
Wine Made
Me Do It

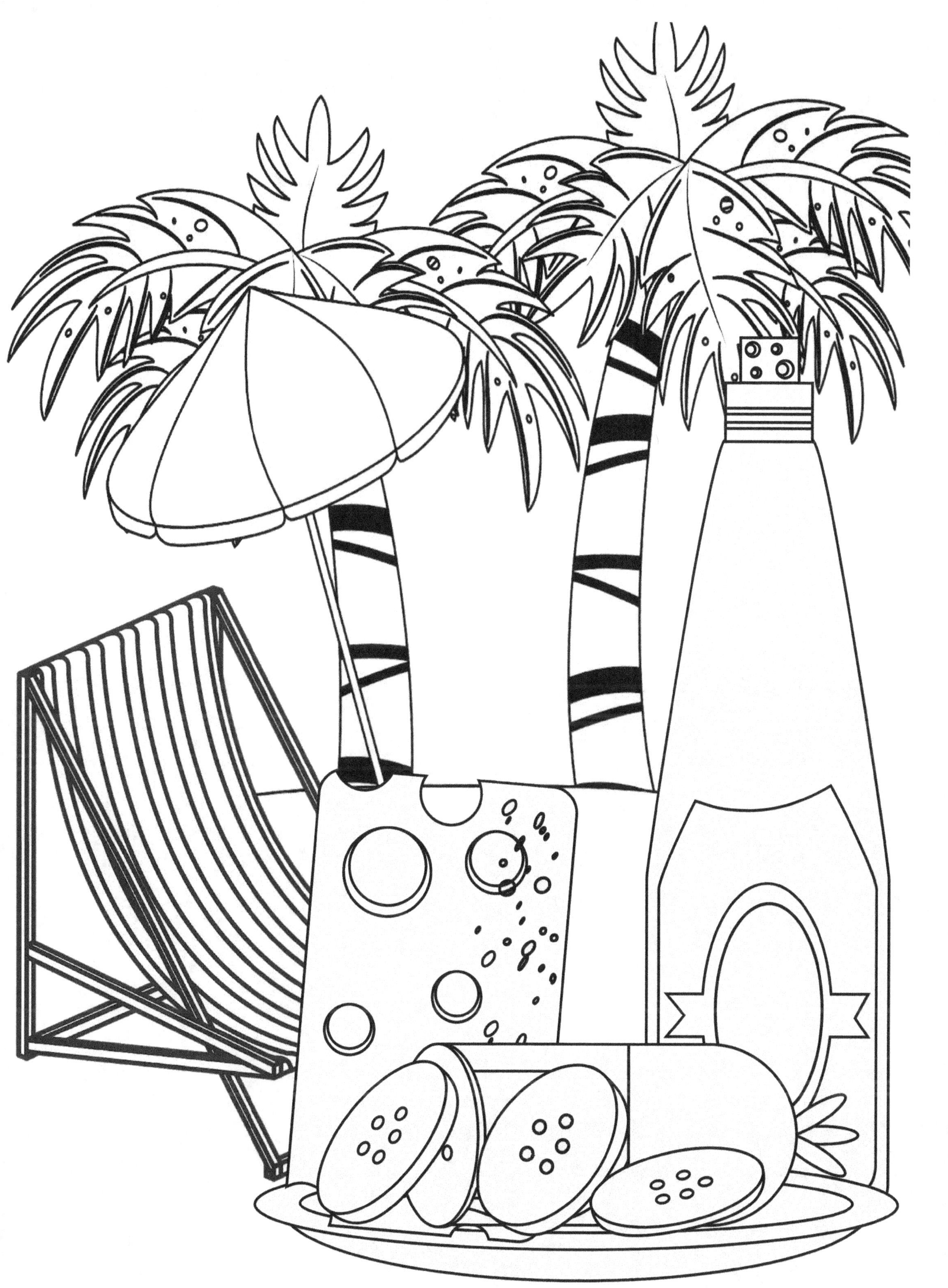

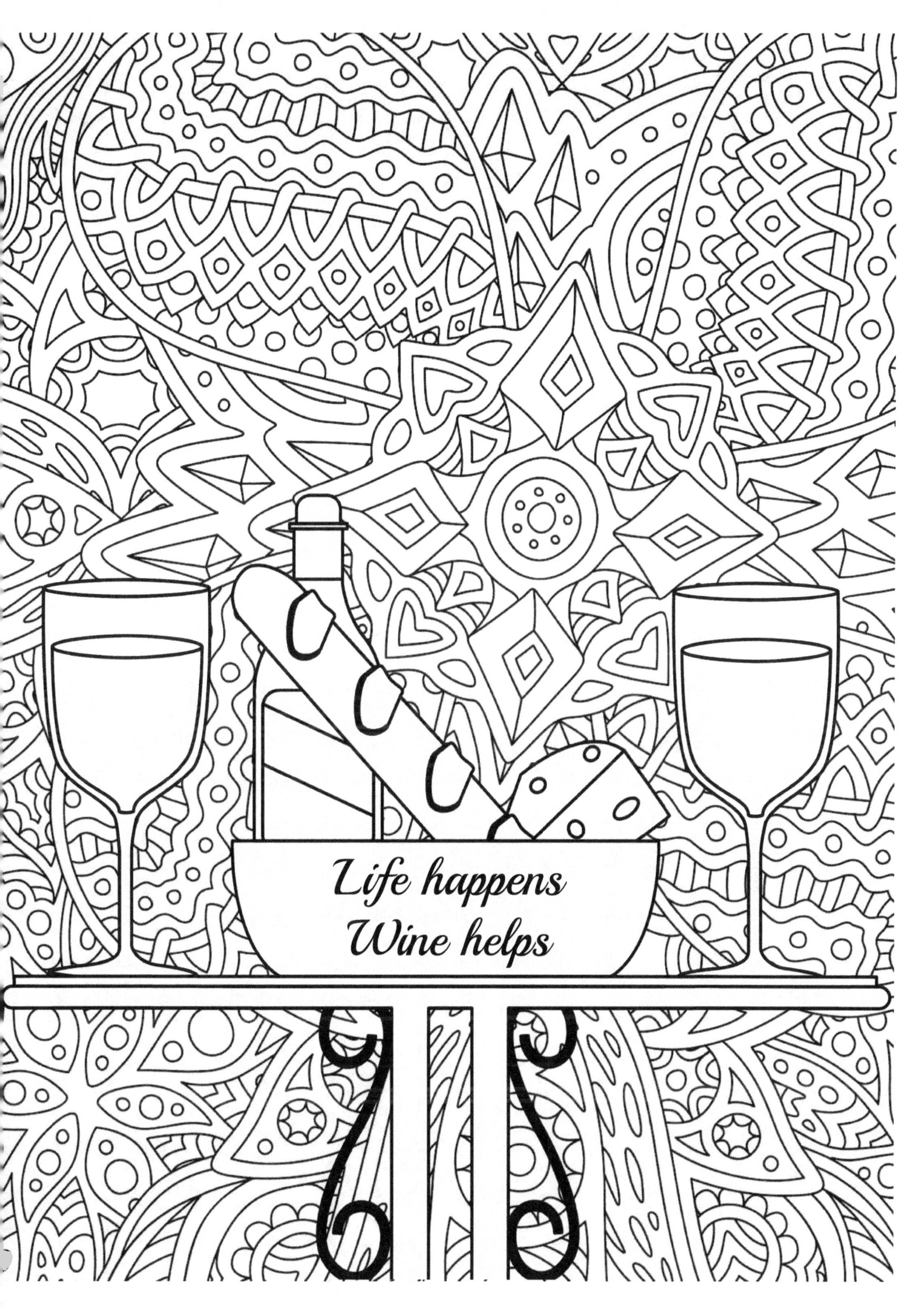

Life happens
Wine helps

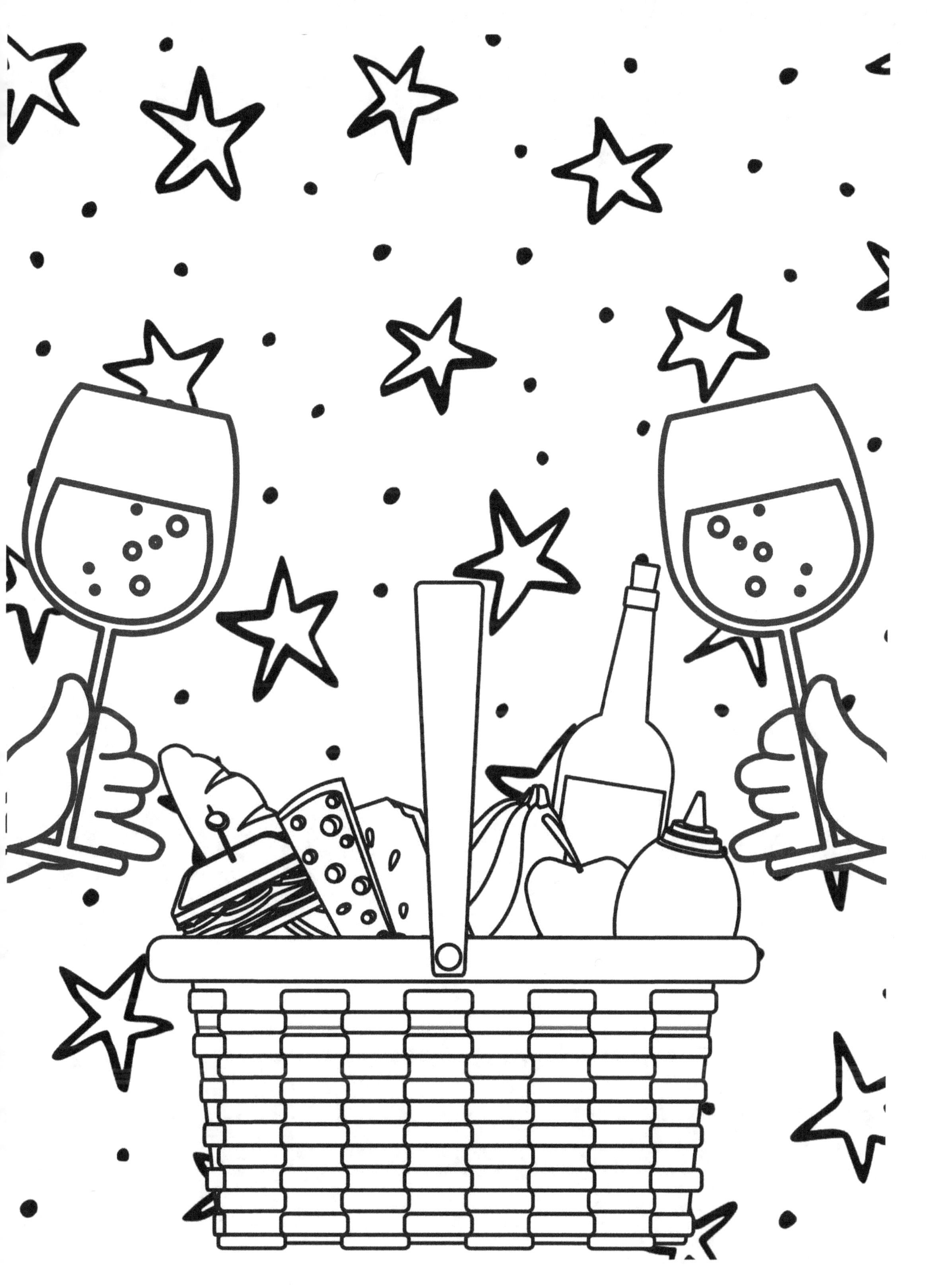

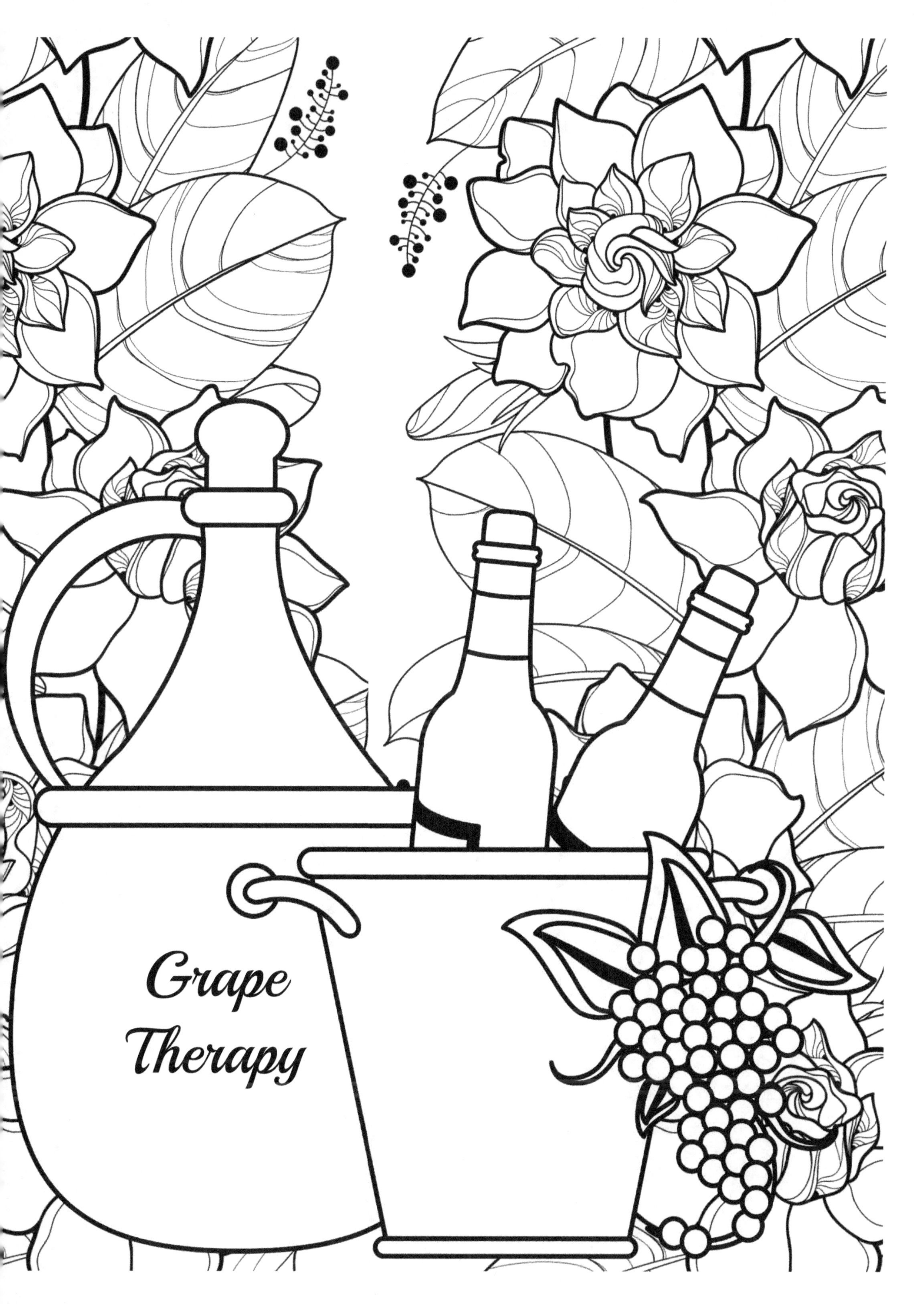

Grape
Therapy

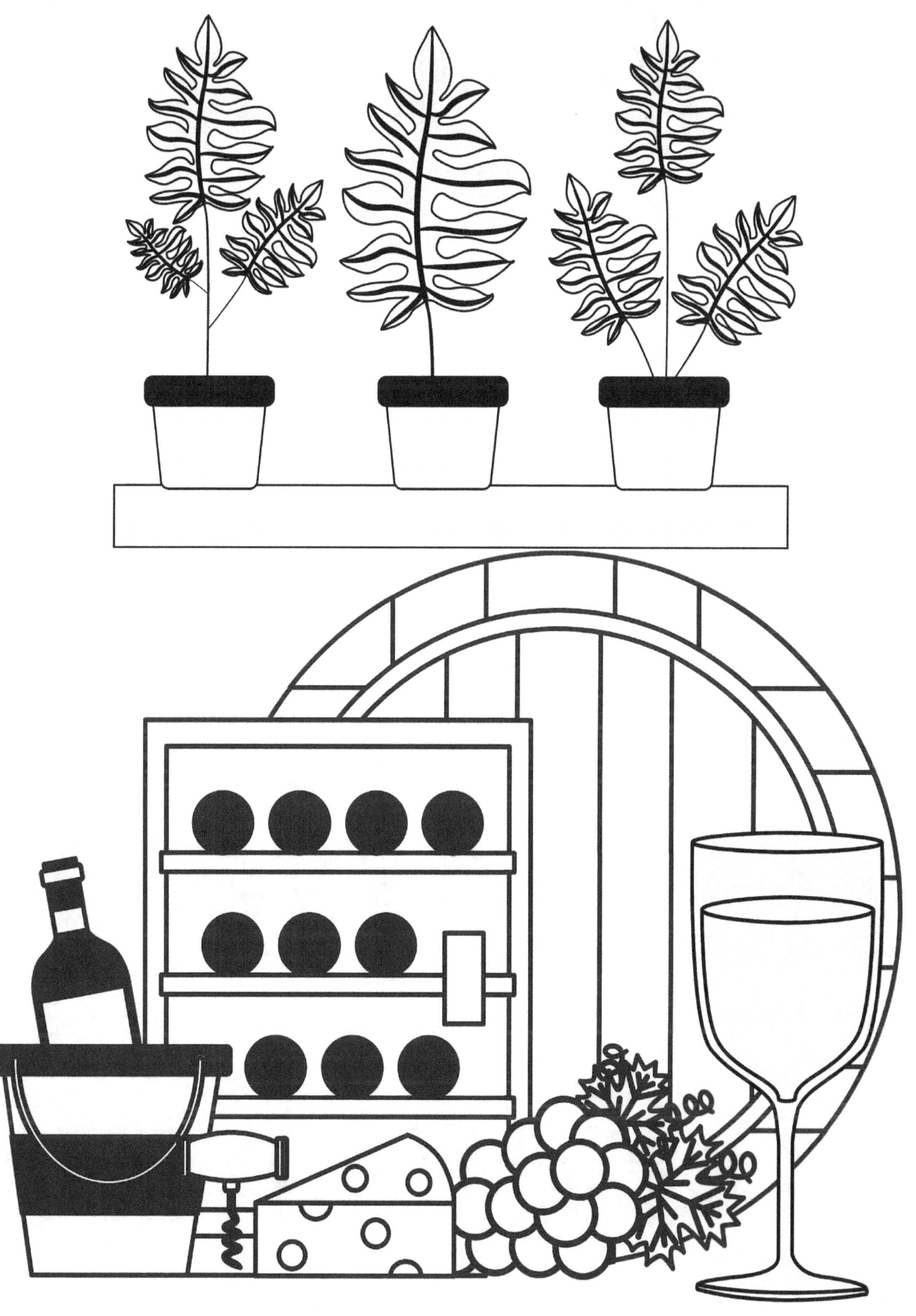

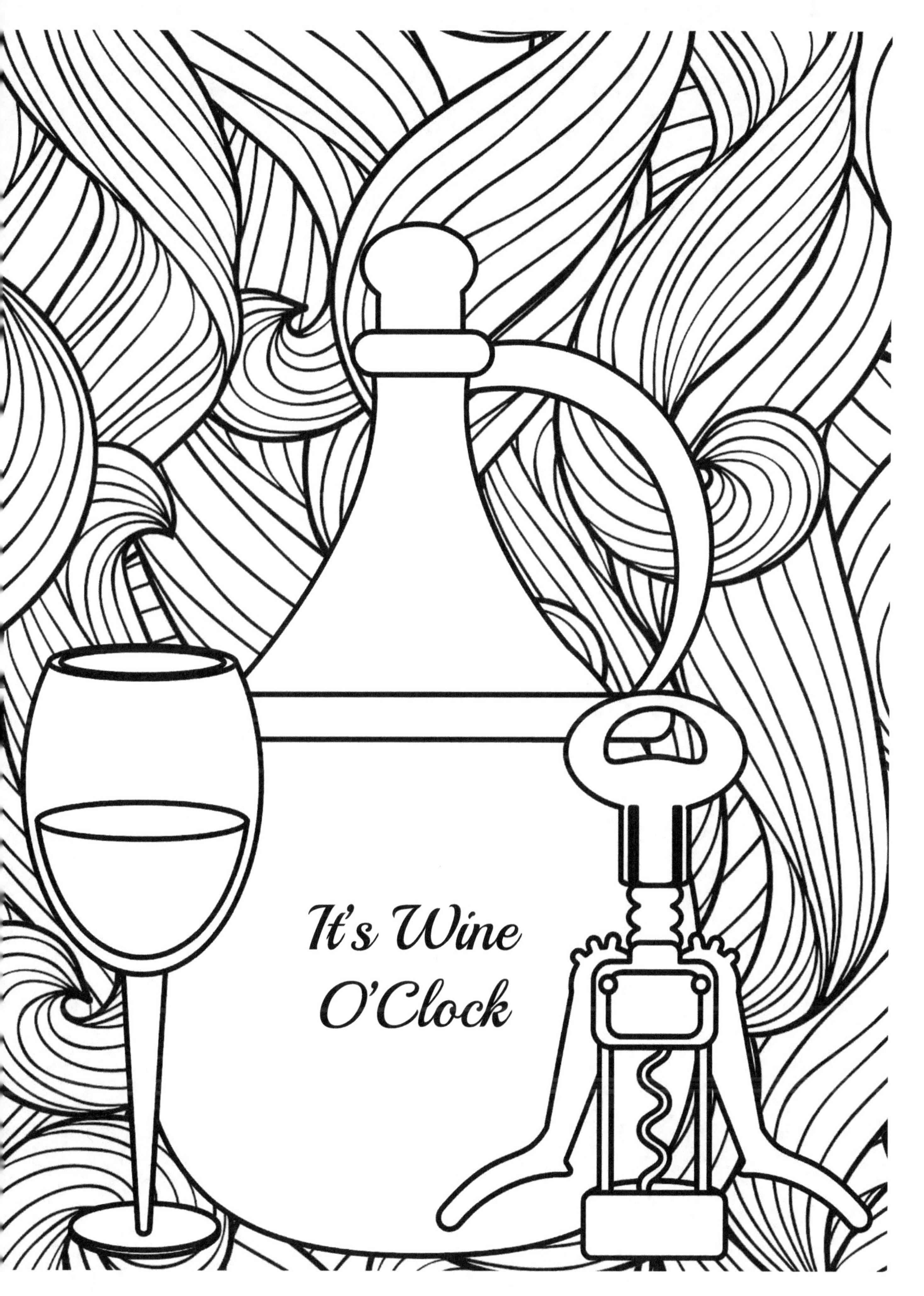

It's Wine
O'Clock

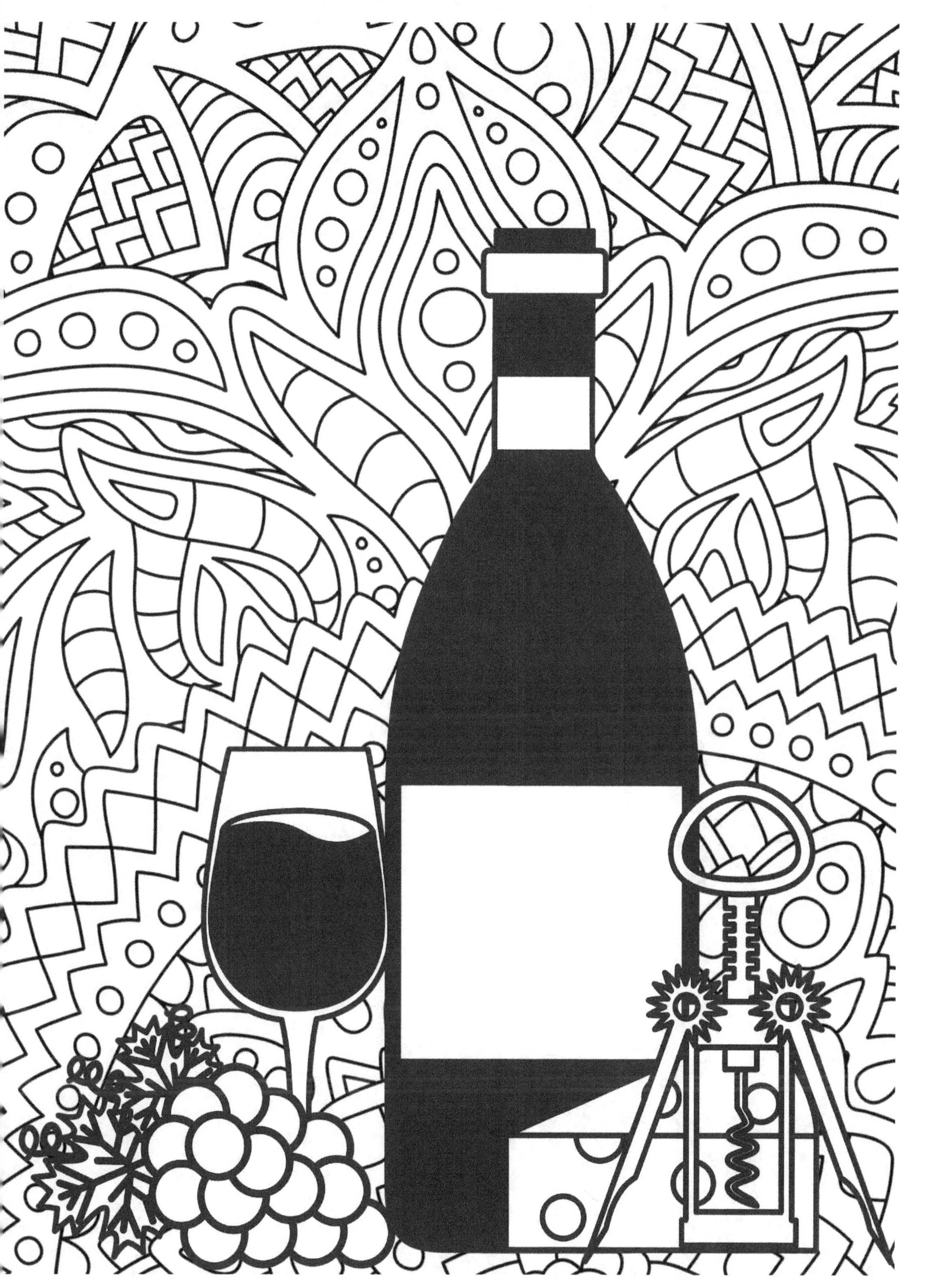

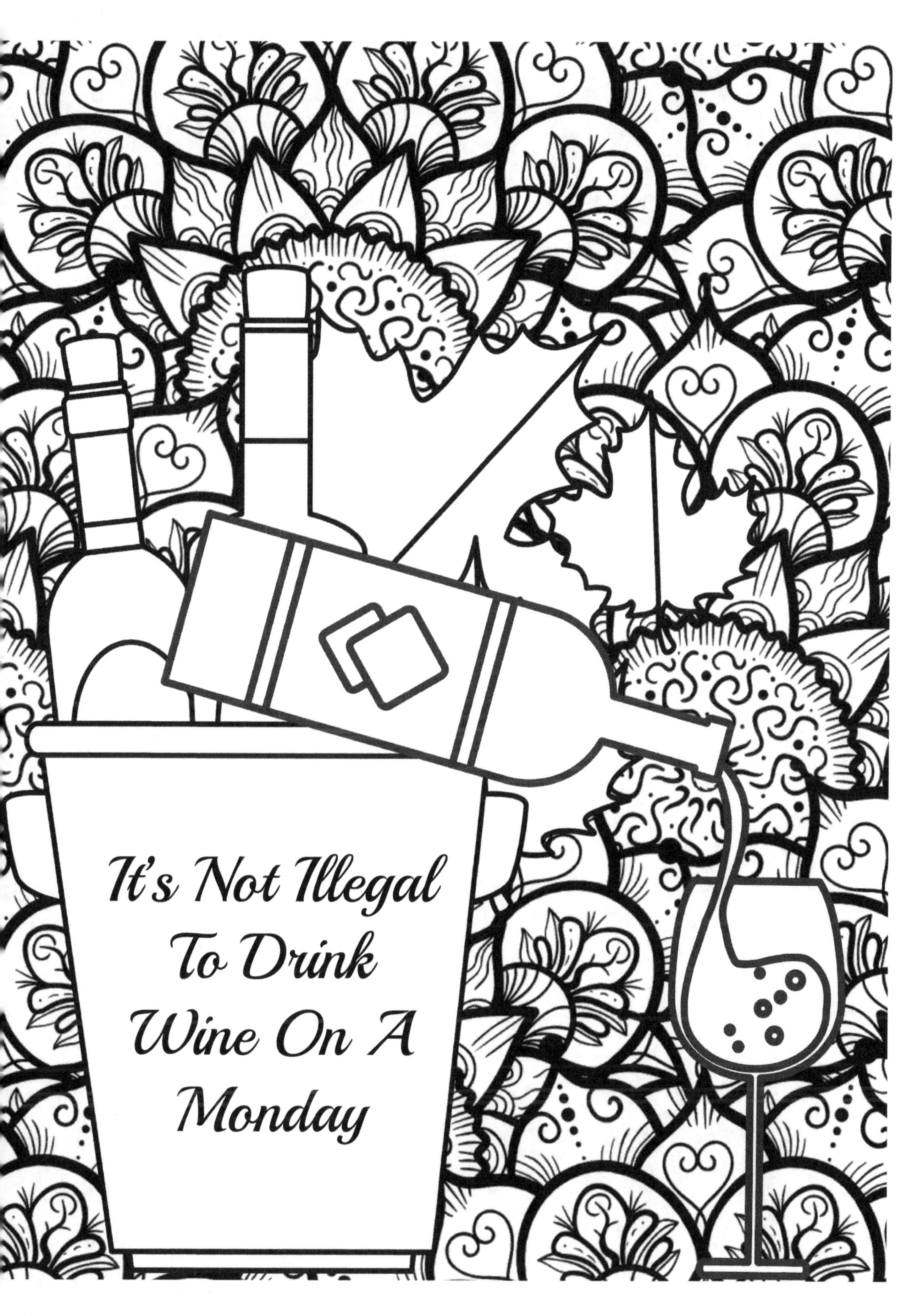

It's Not Illegal
To Drink
Wine On A
Monday

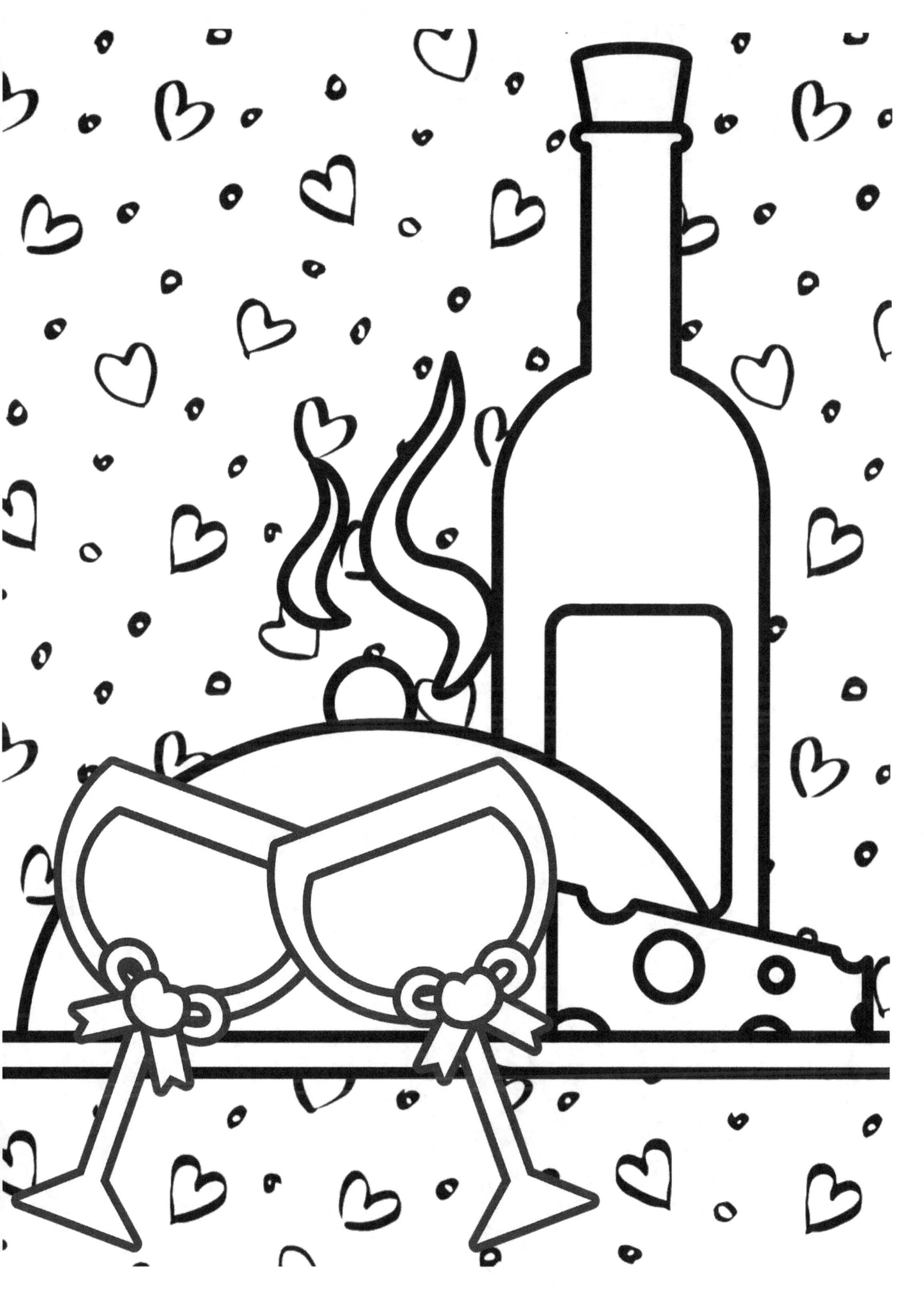

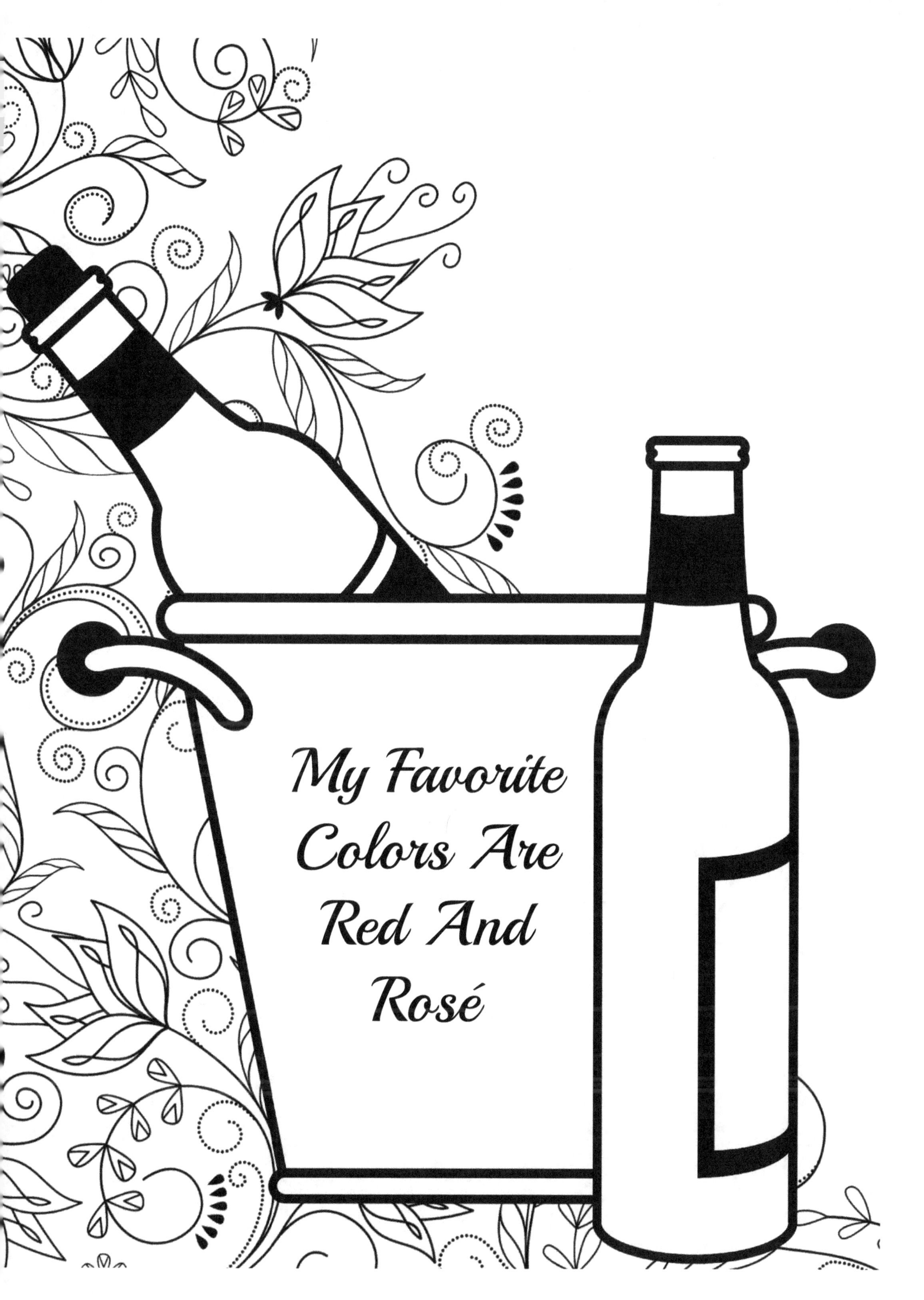

My Favorite
Colors Are
Red And
Rosé

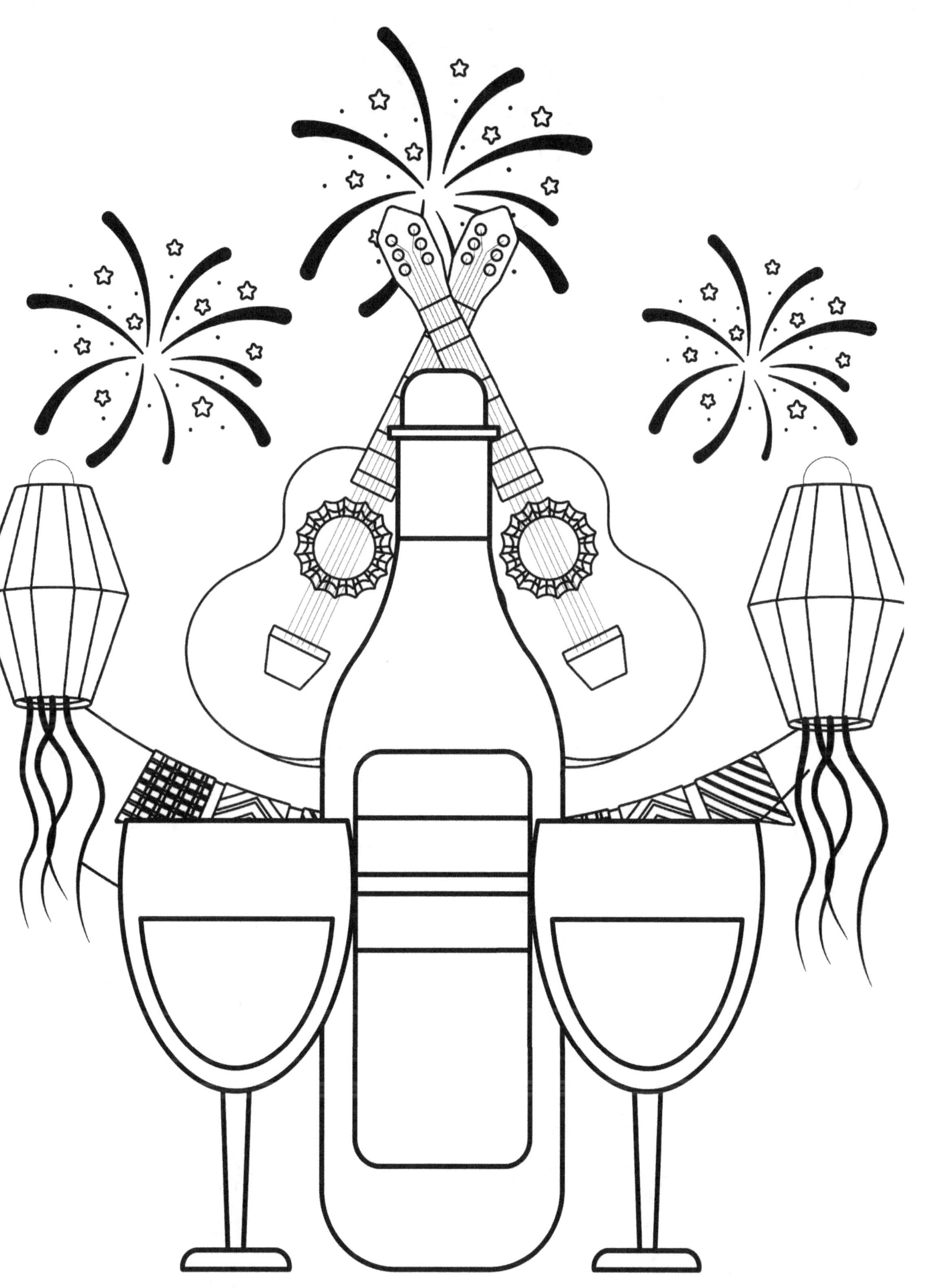

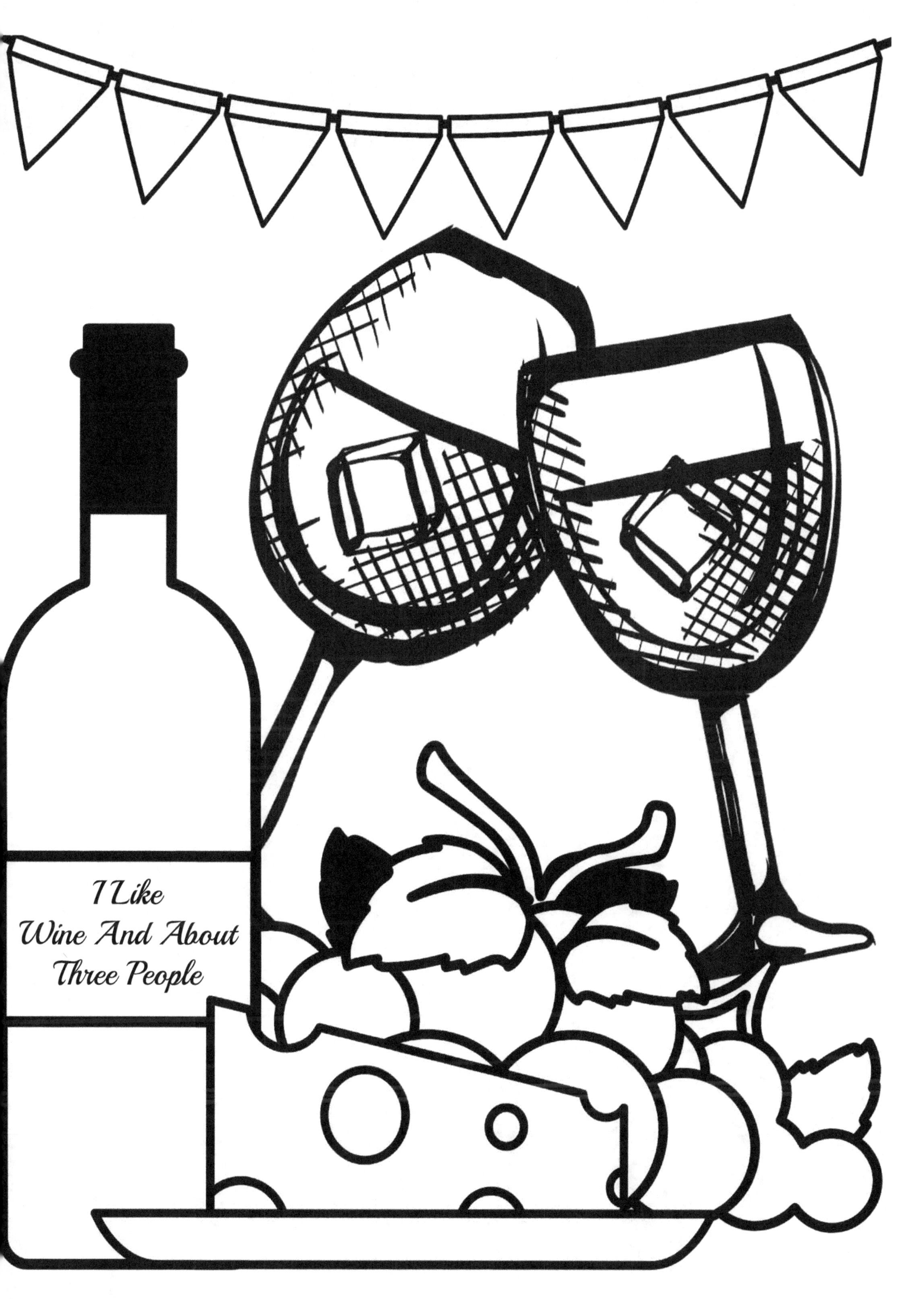

I Like
Wine And About
Three People

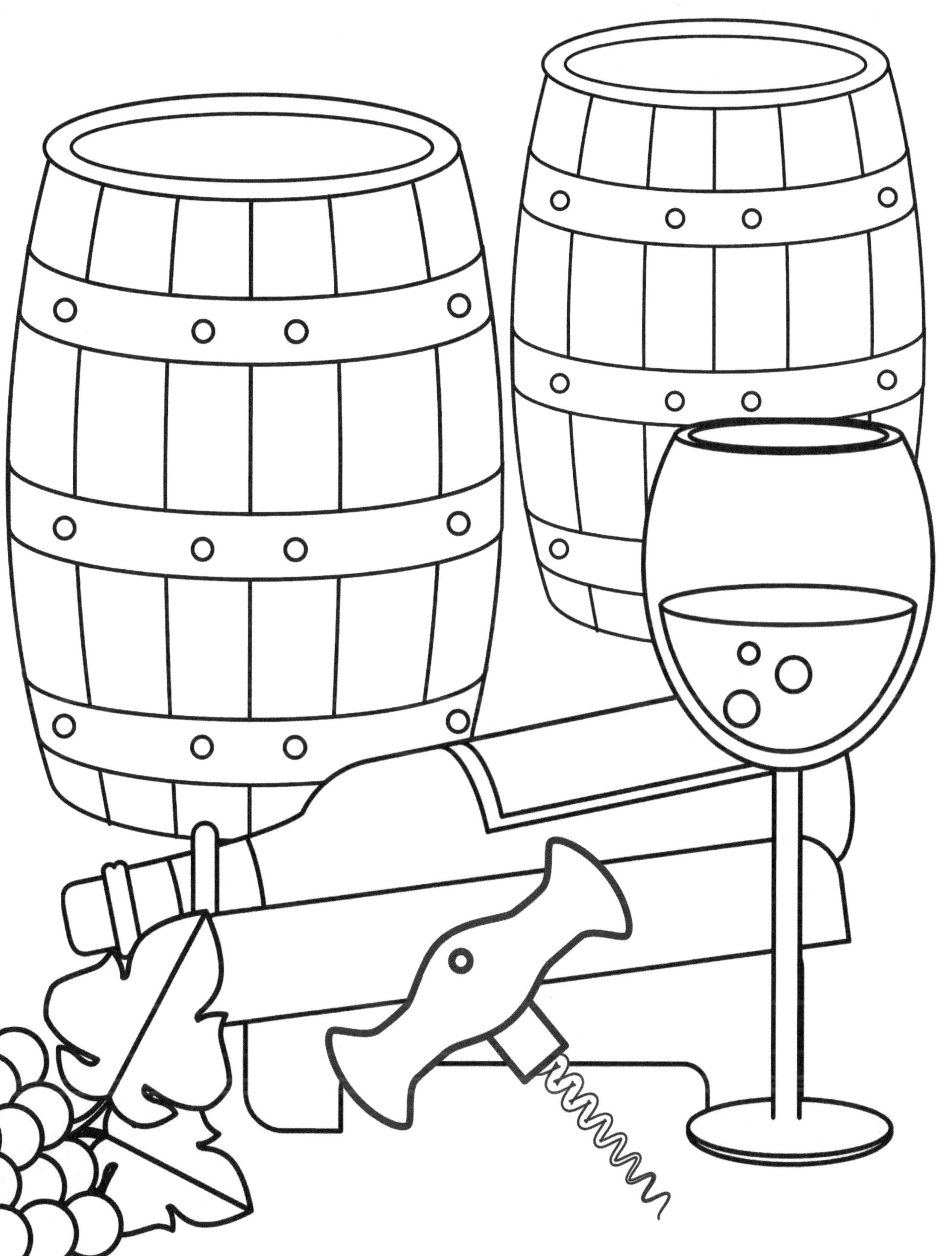

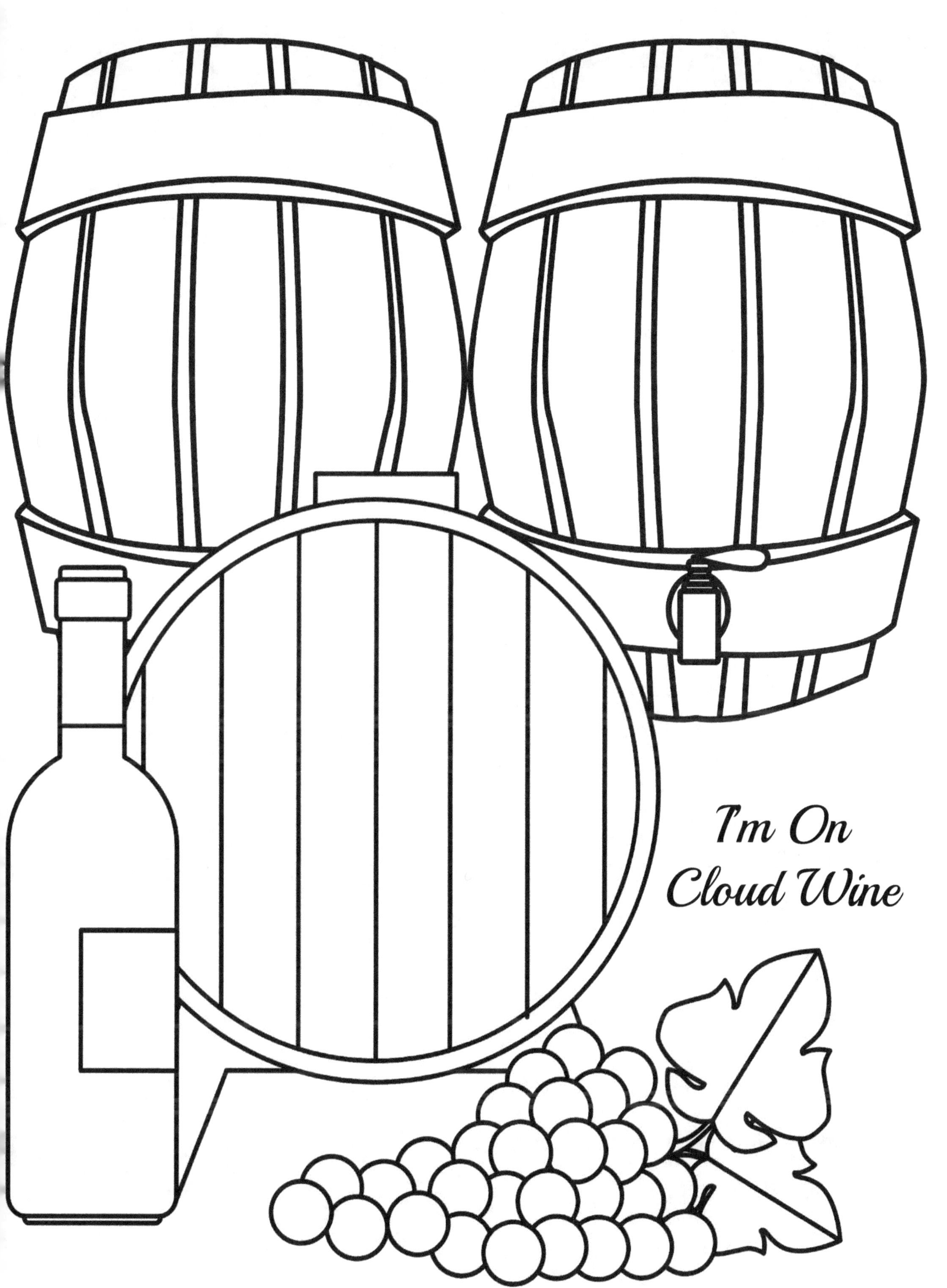

I'm On
Cloud Wine

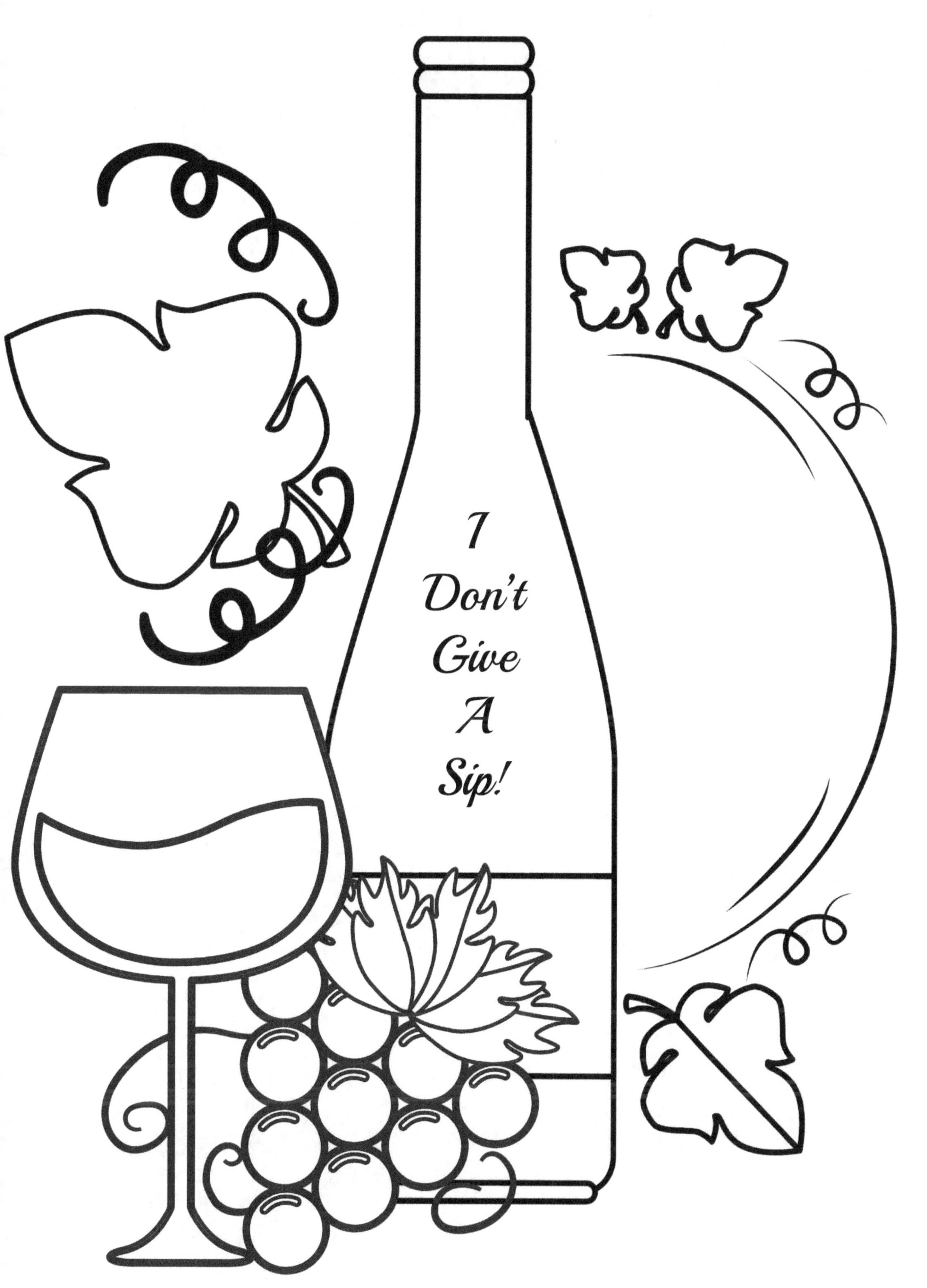

I
Don't
Give
A
Sip!

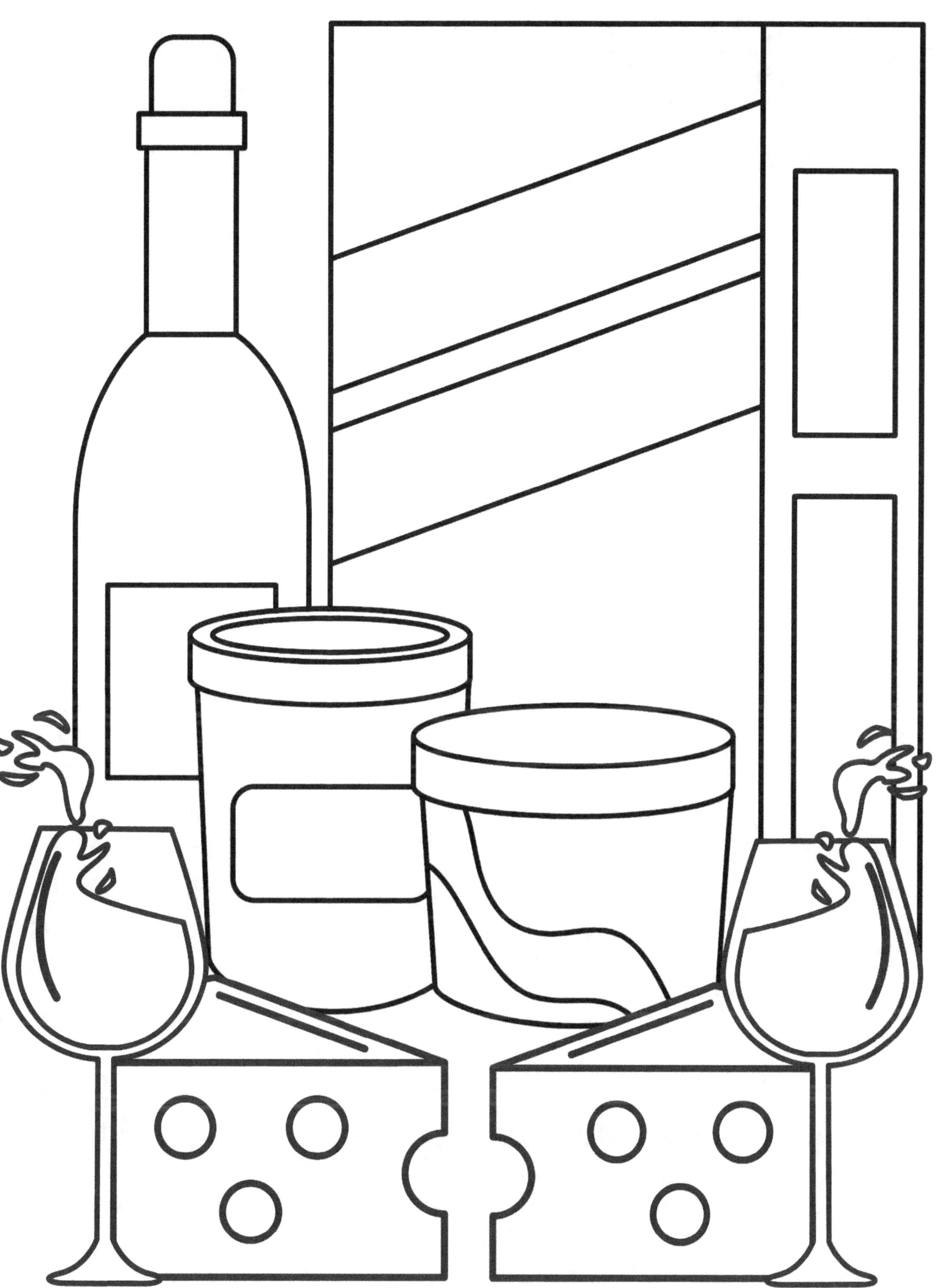

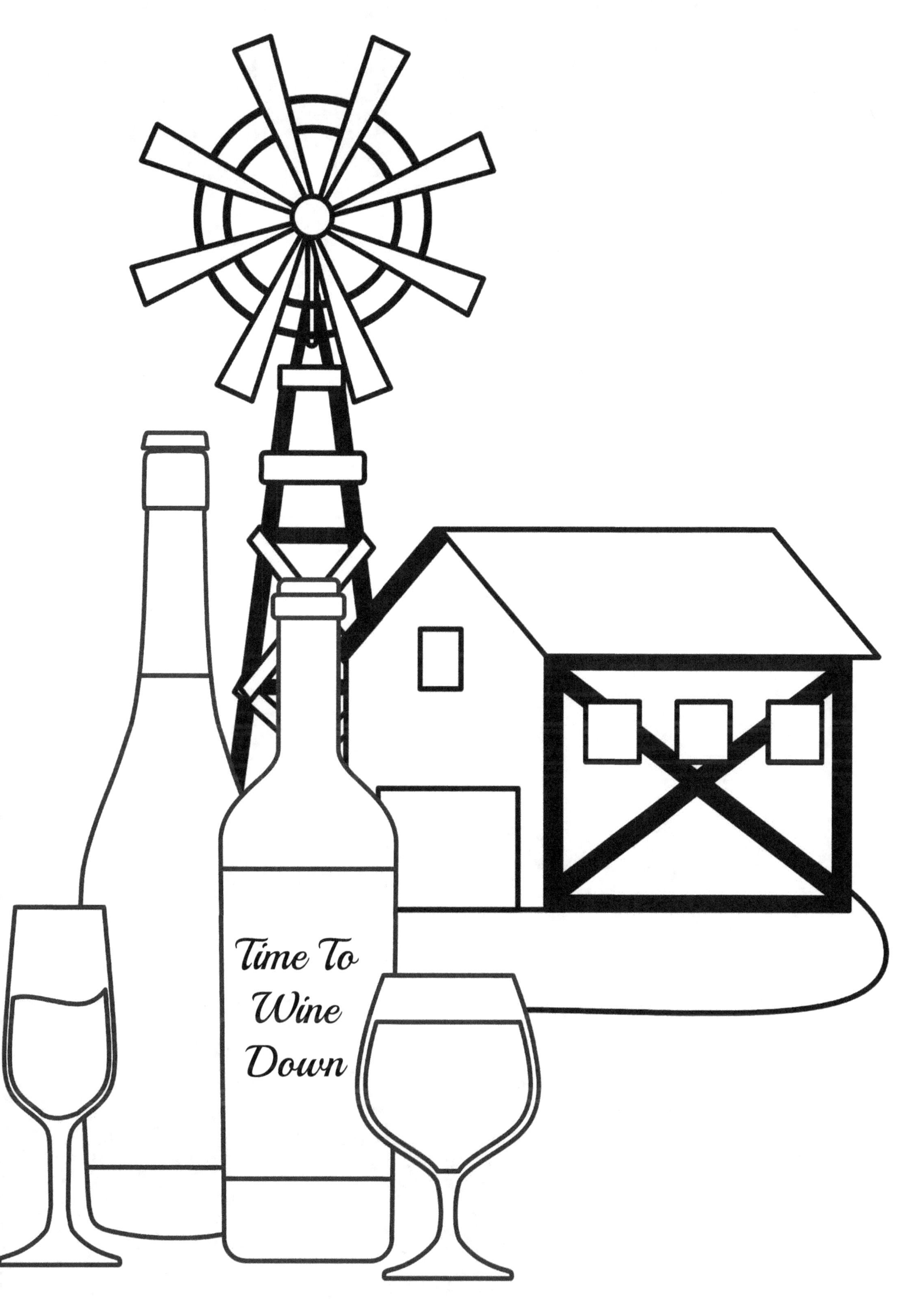

Time To
Wine
Down

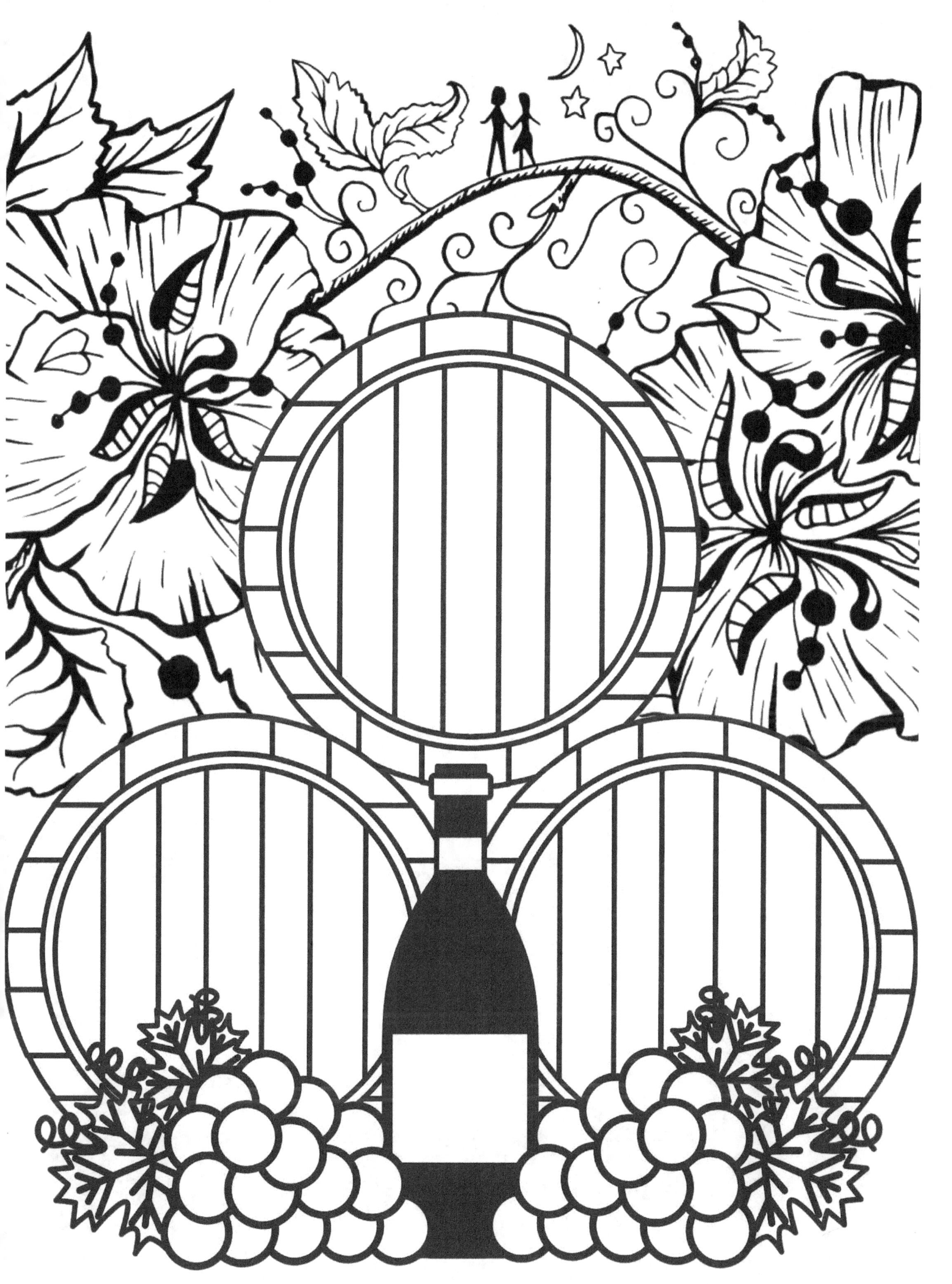

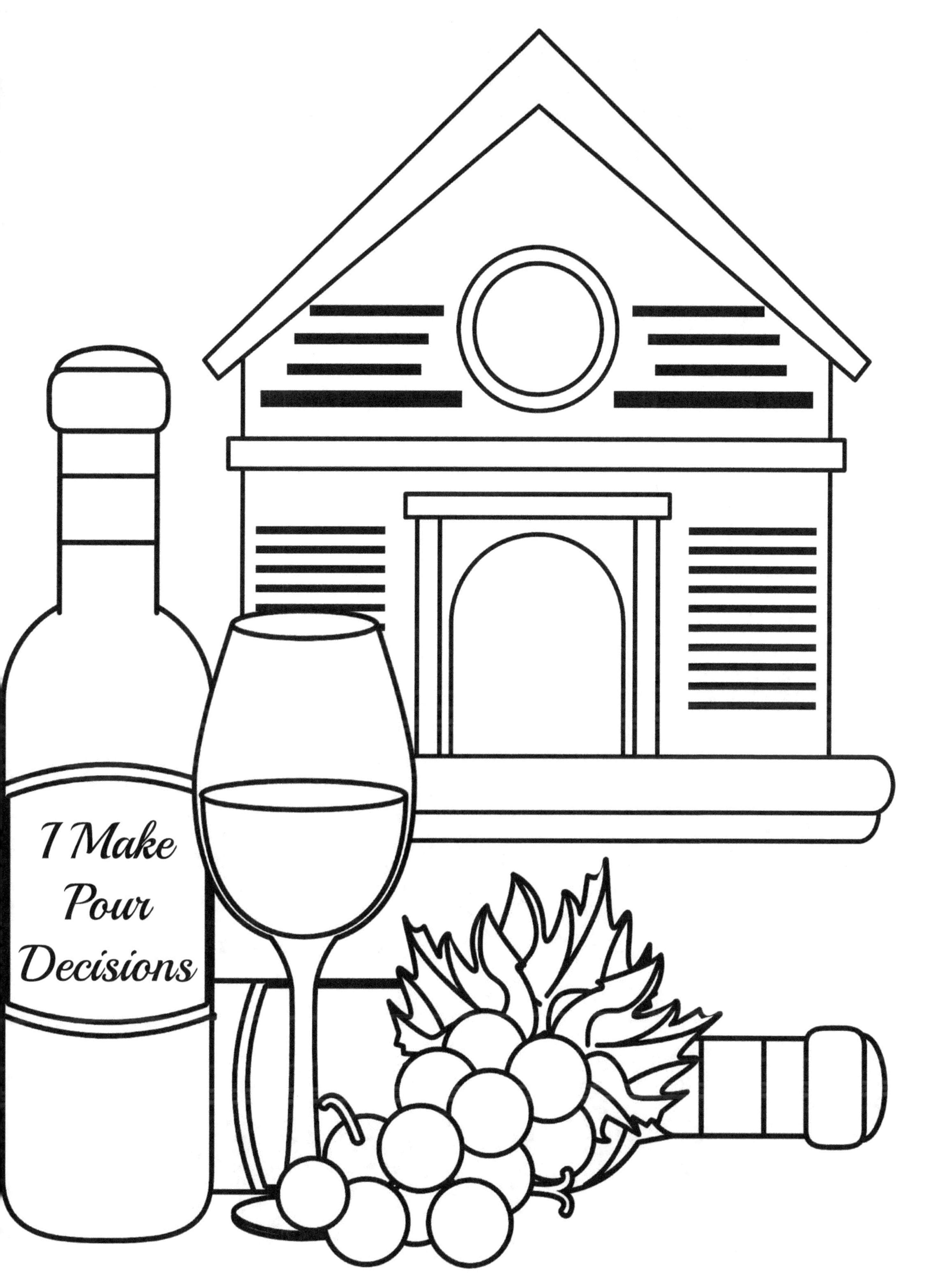

I Make
Pour
Decisions

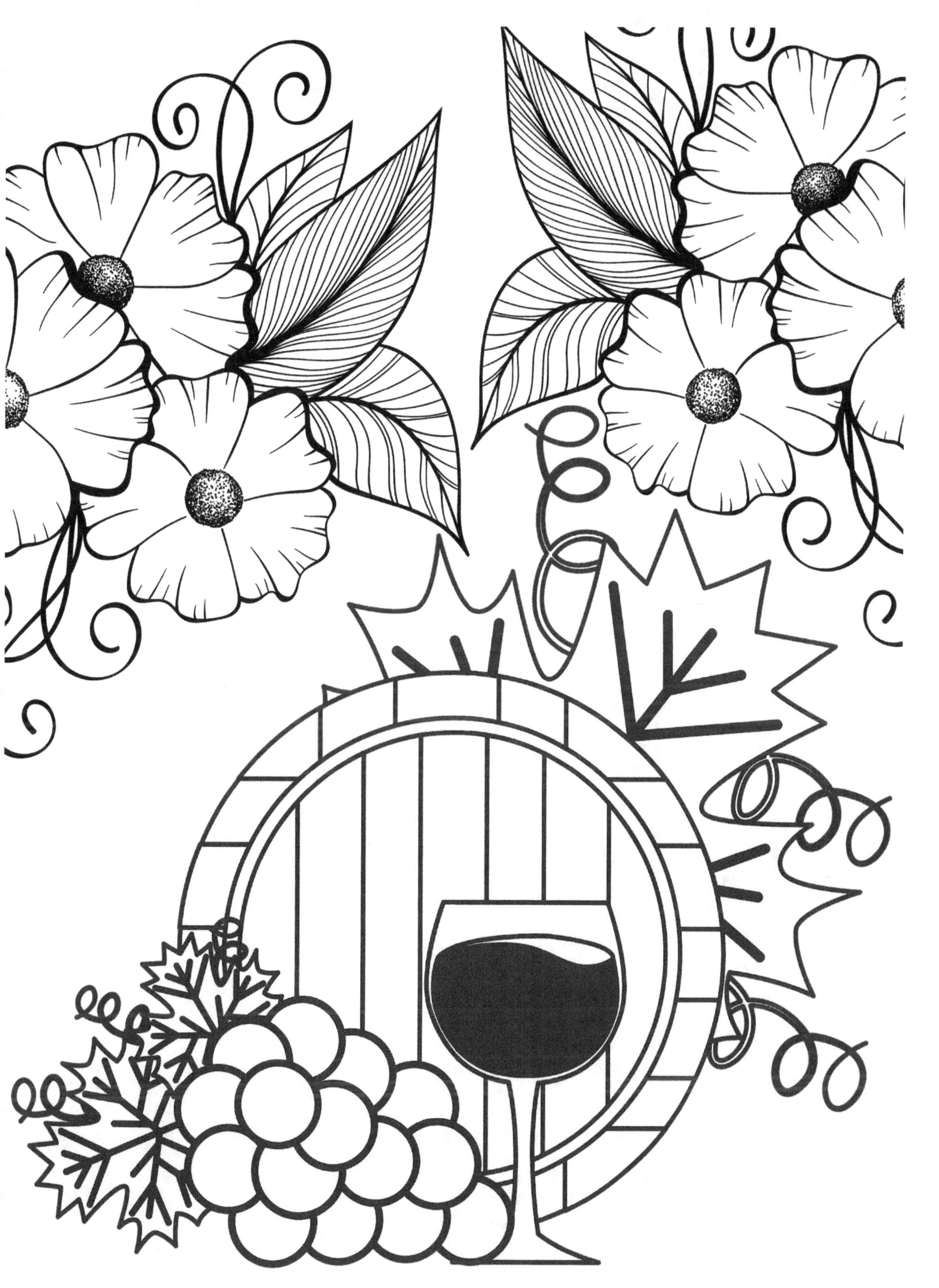

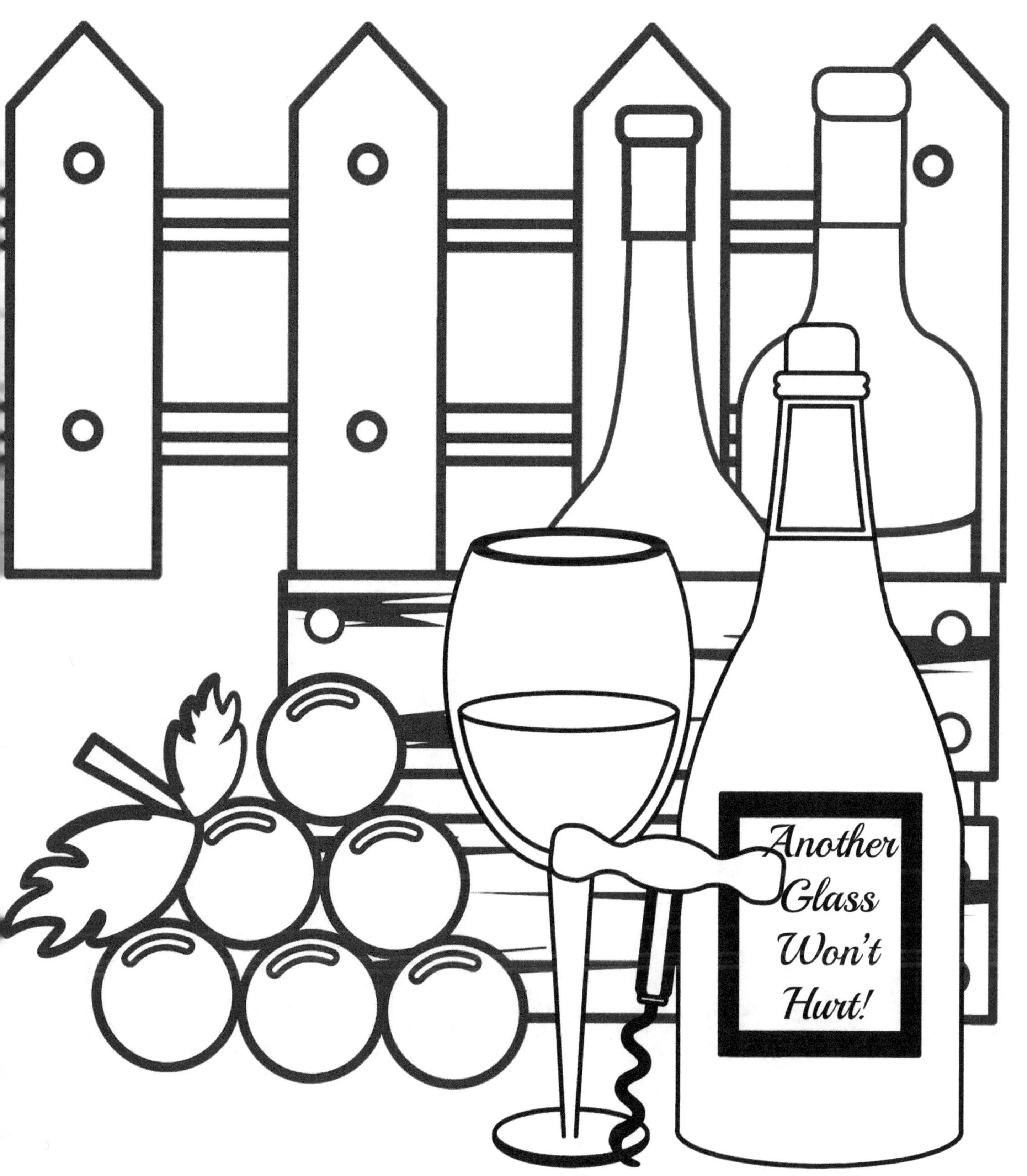

Another
Glass
Won't
Hurt!

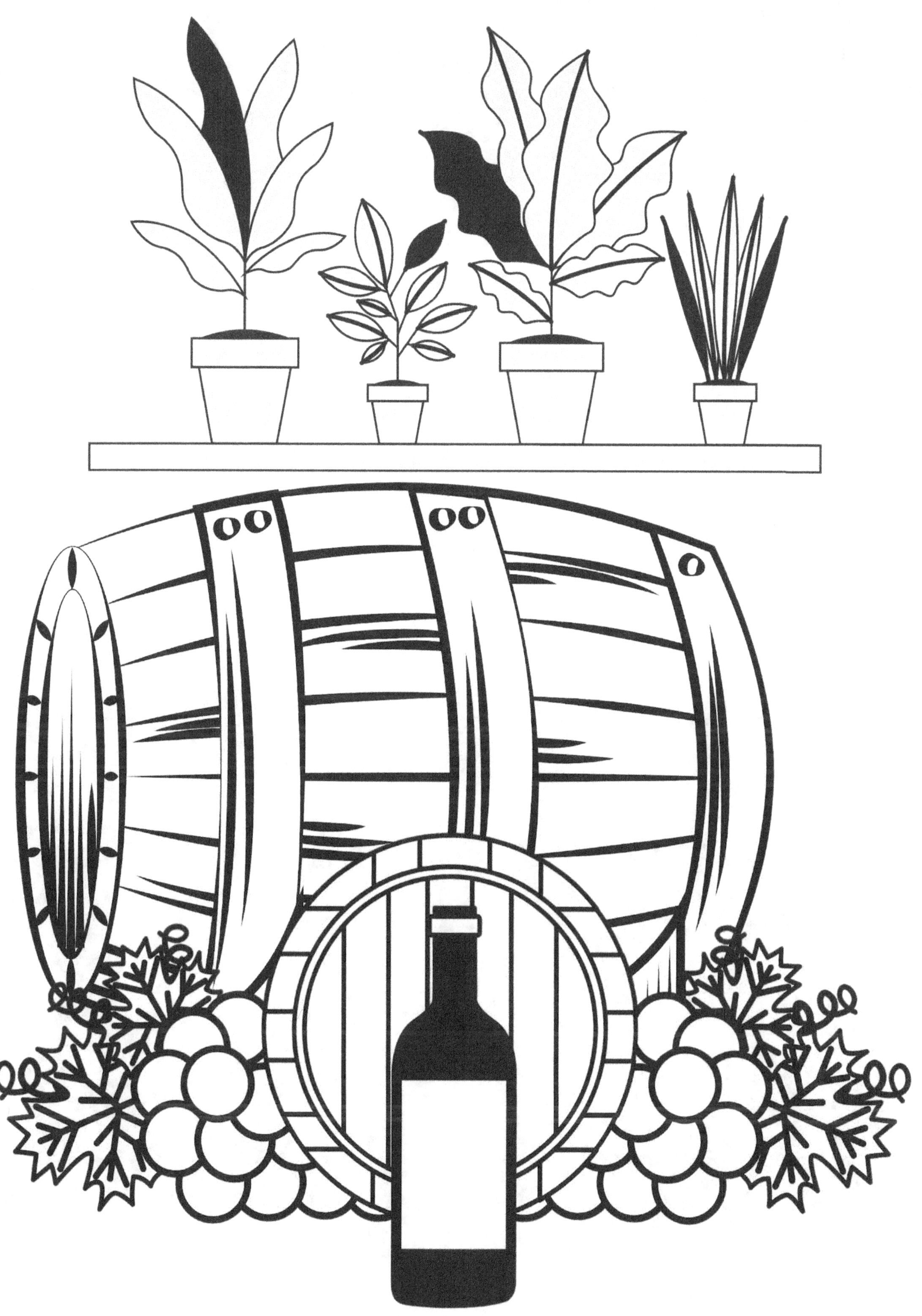

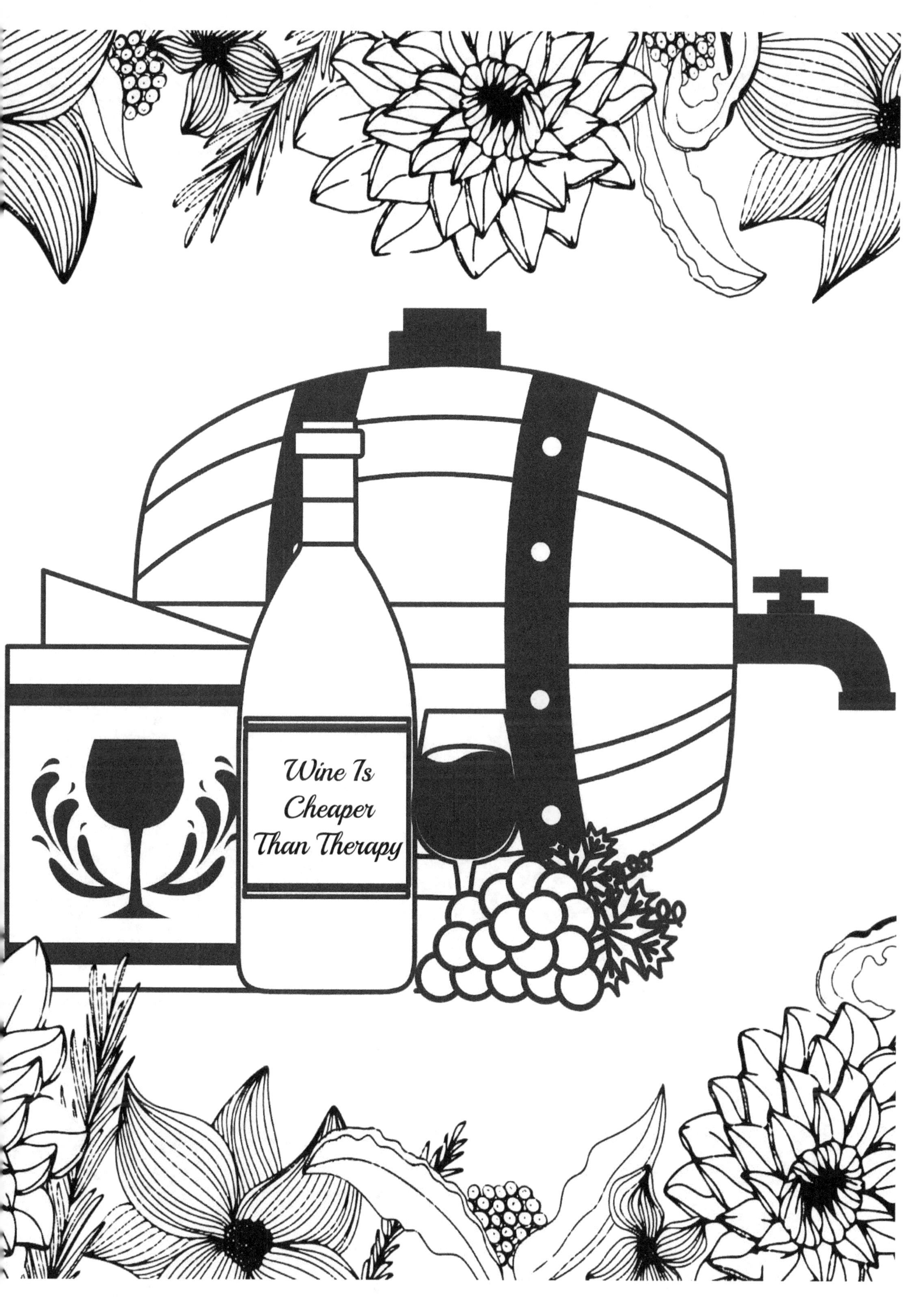

Wine Is
Cheaper
Than Therapy

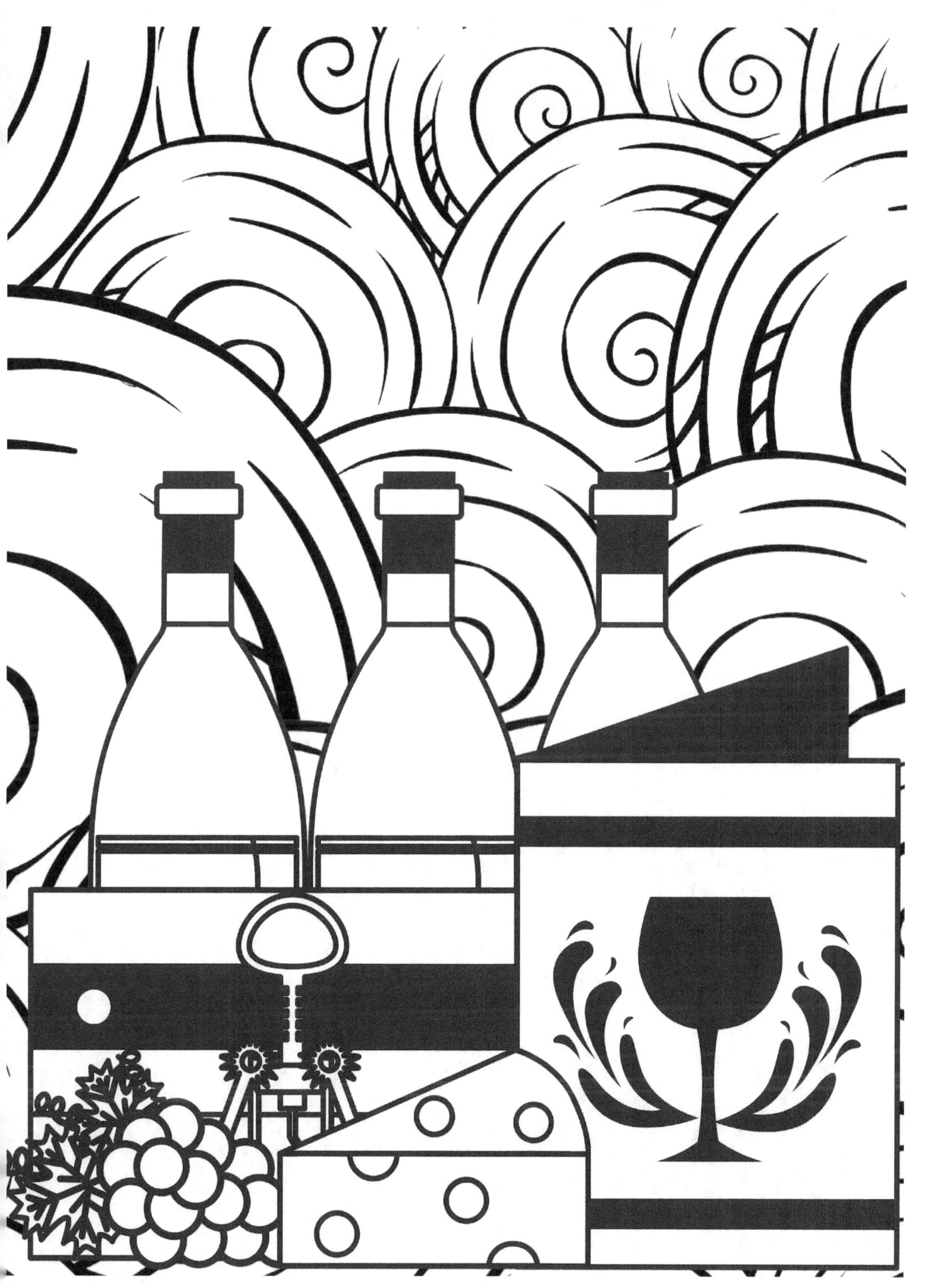

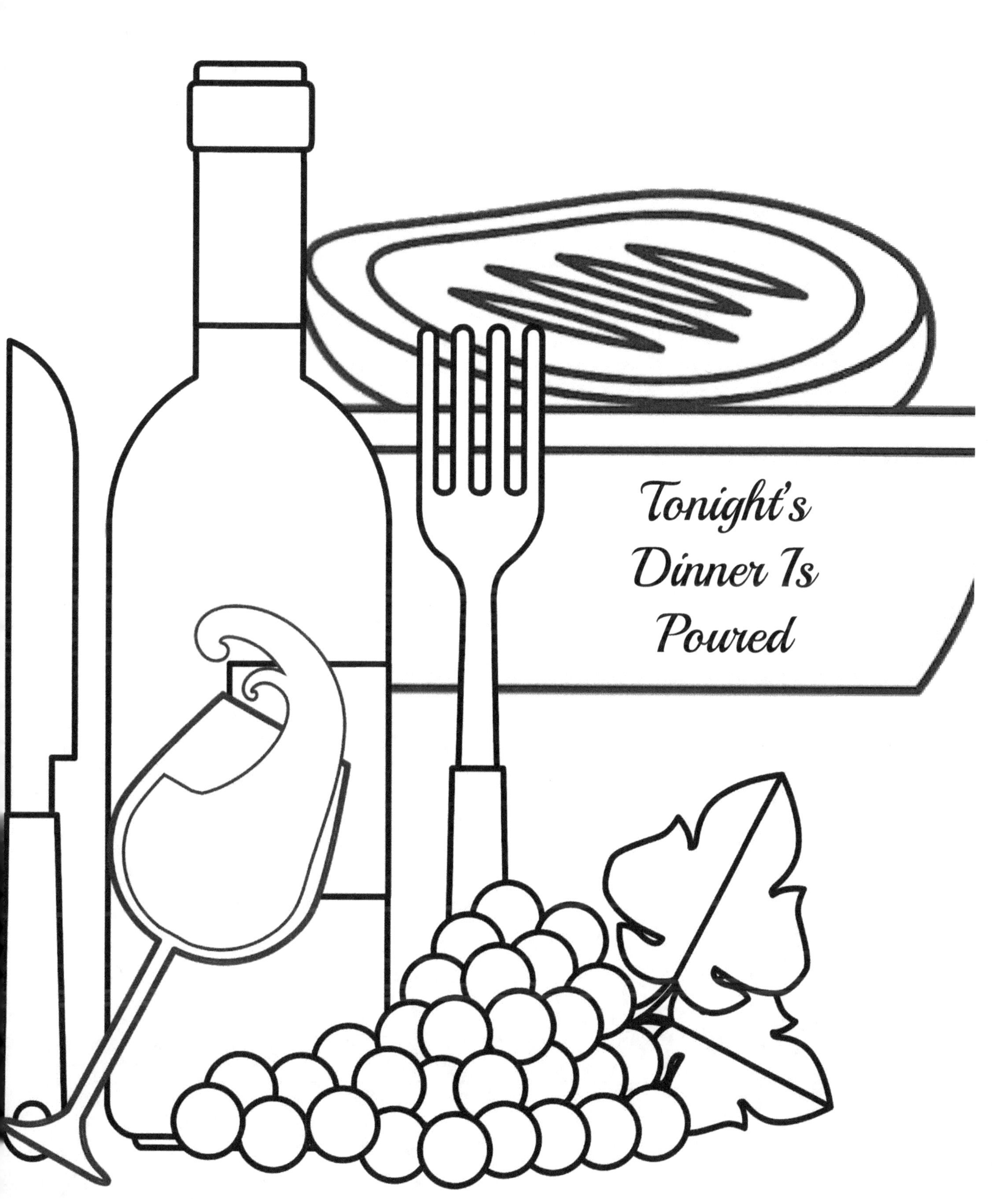

Tonight's
Dinner Is
Poured

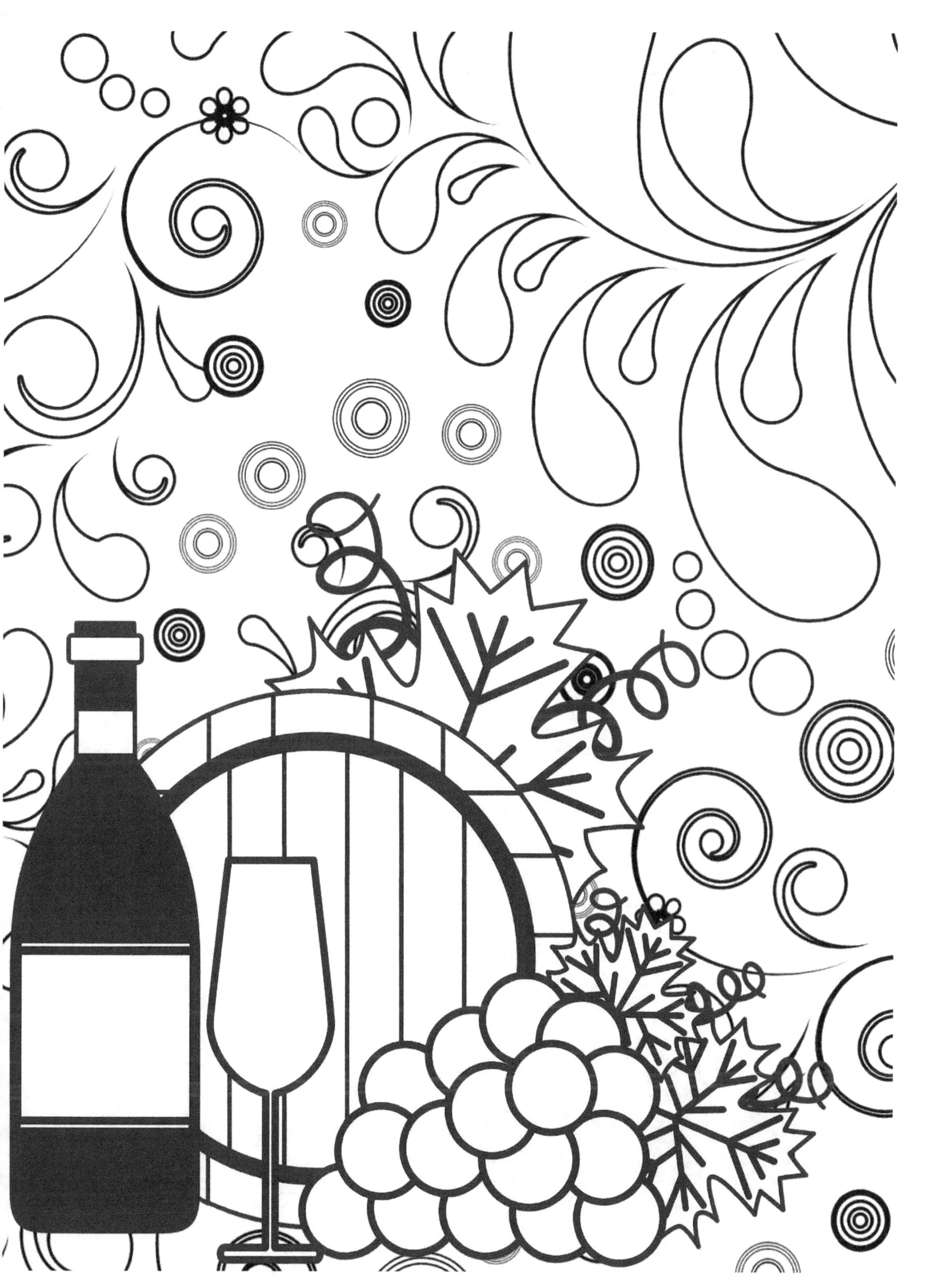

I Don't
Whine,
I Wine.

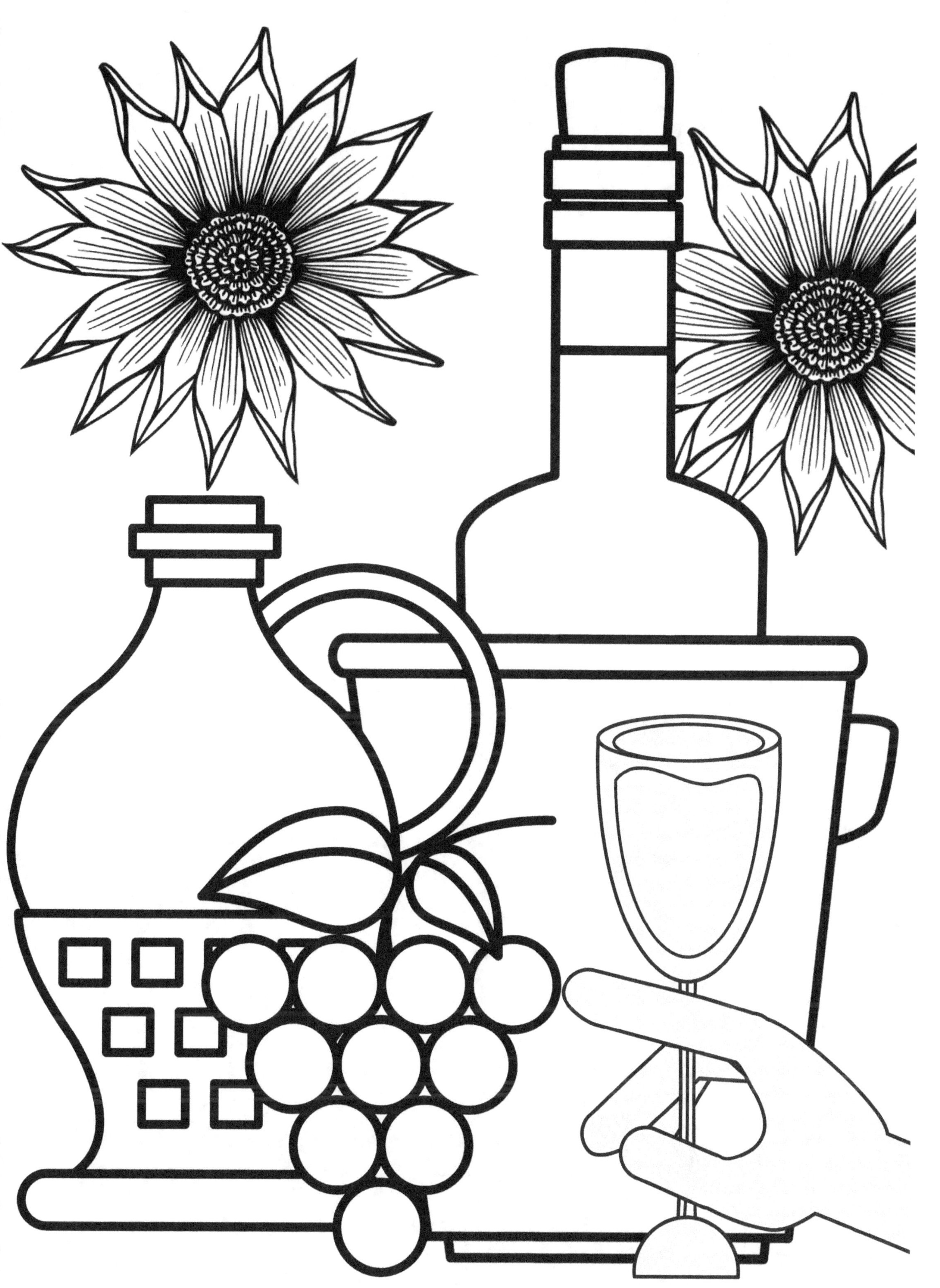

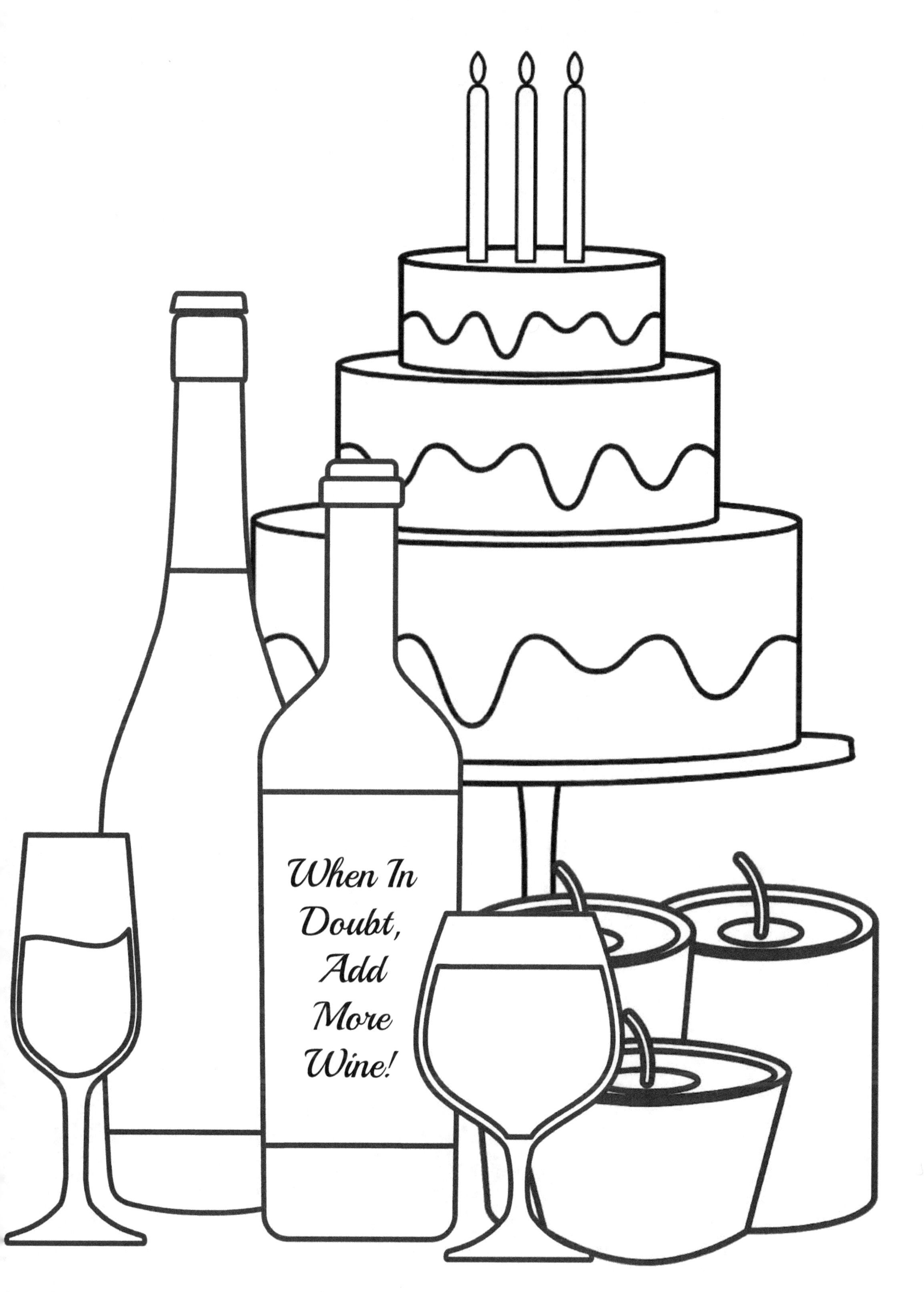
When In
Doubt,
Add
More
Wine!

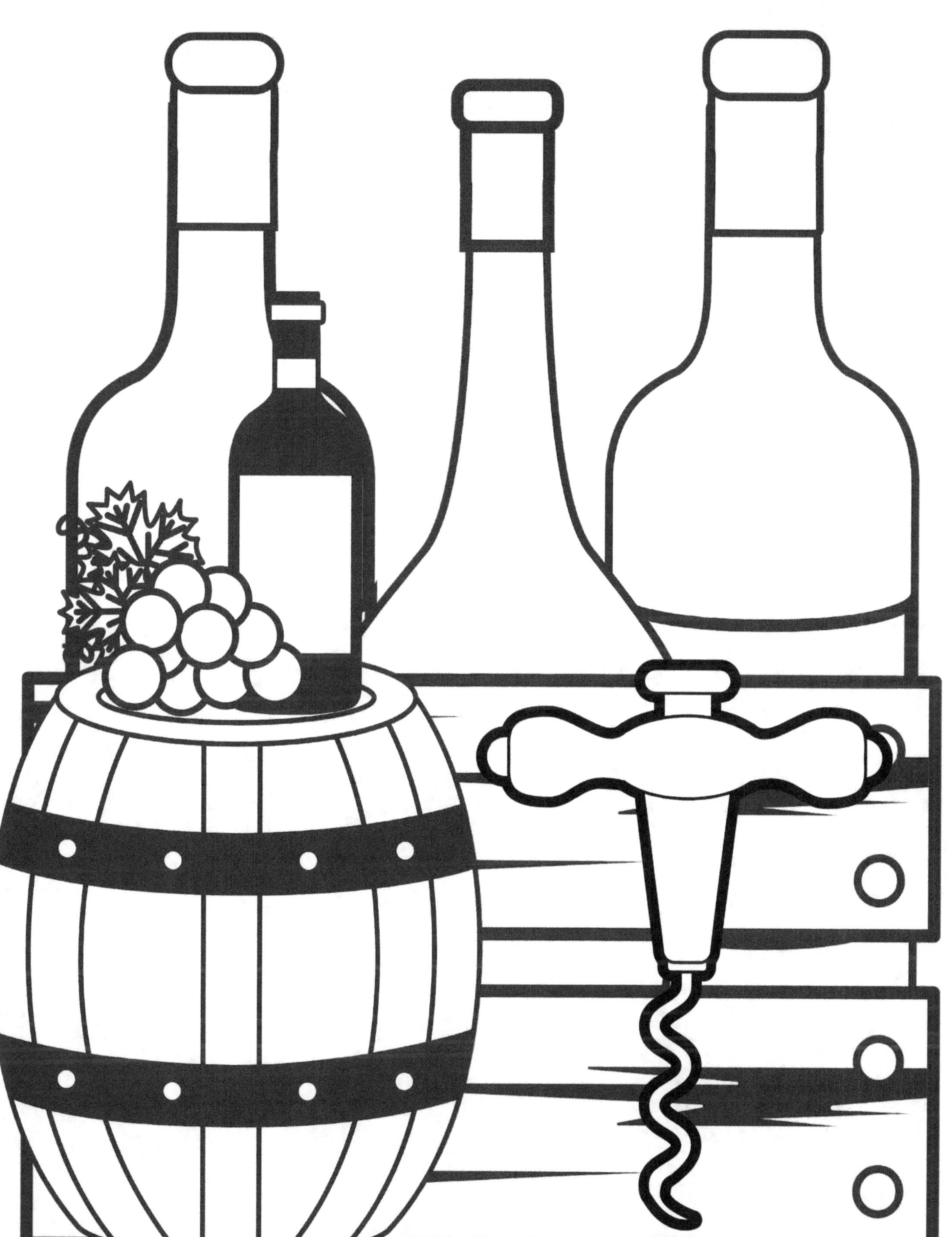

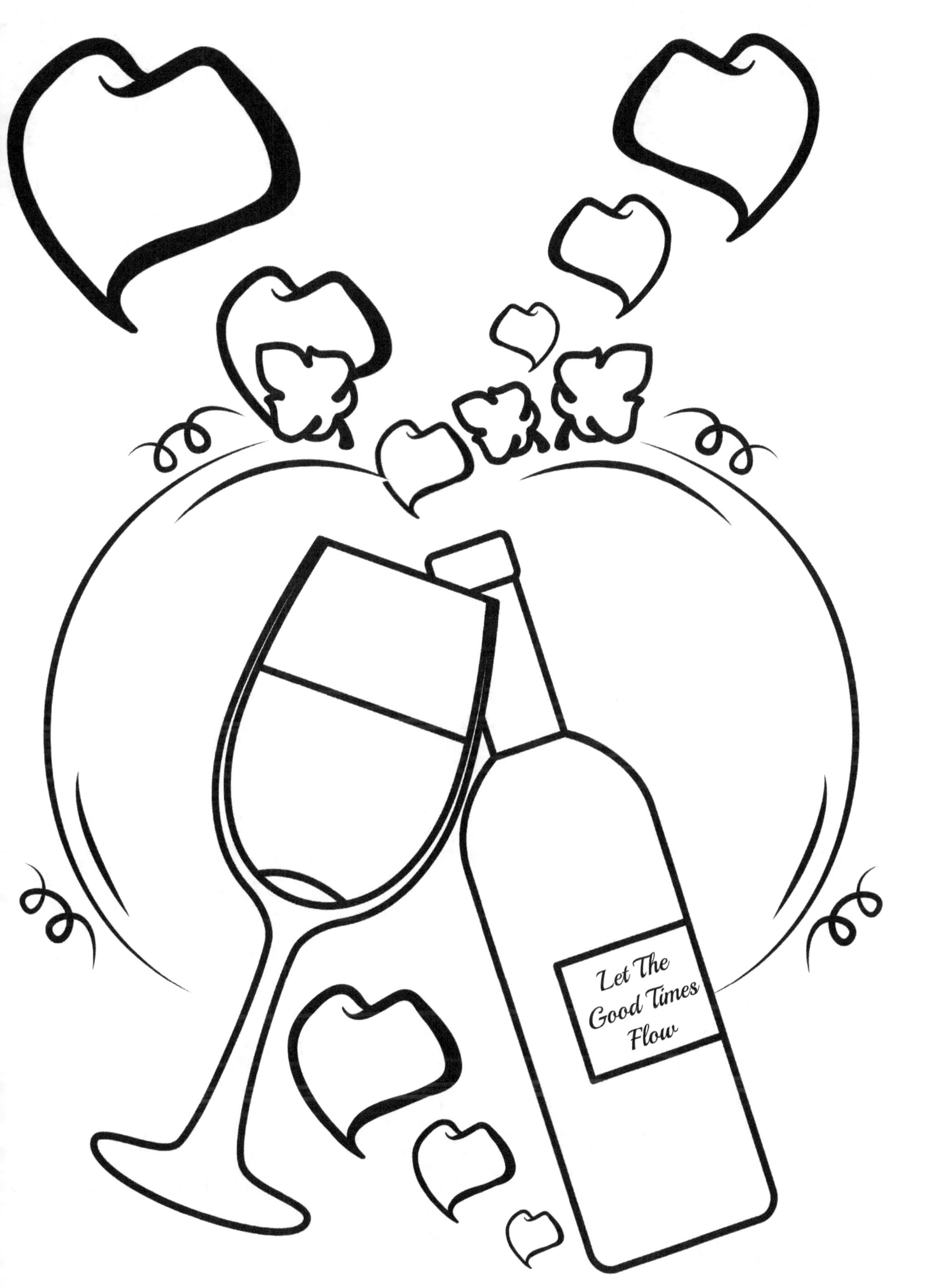

Let The
Good Times
Flow

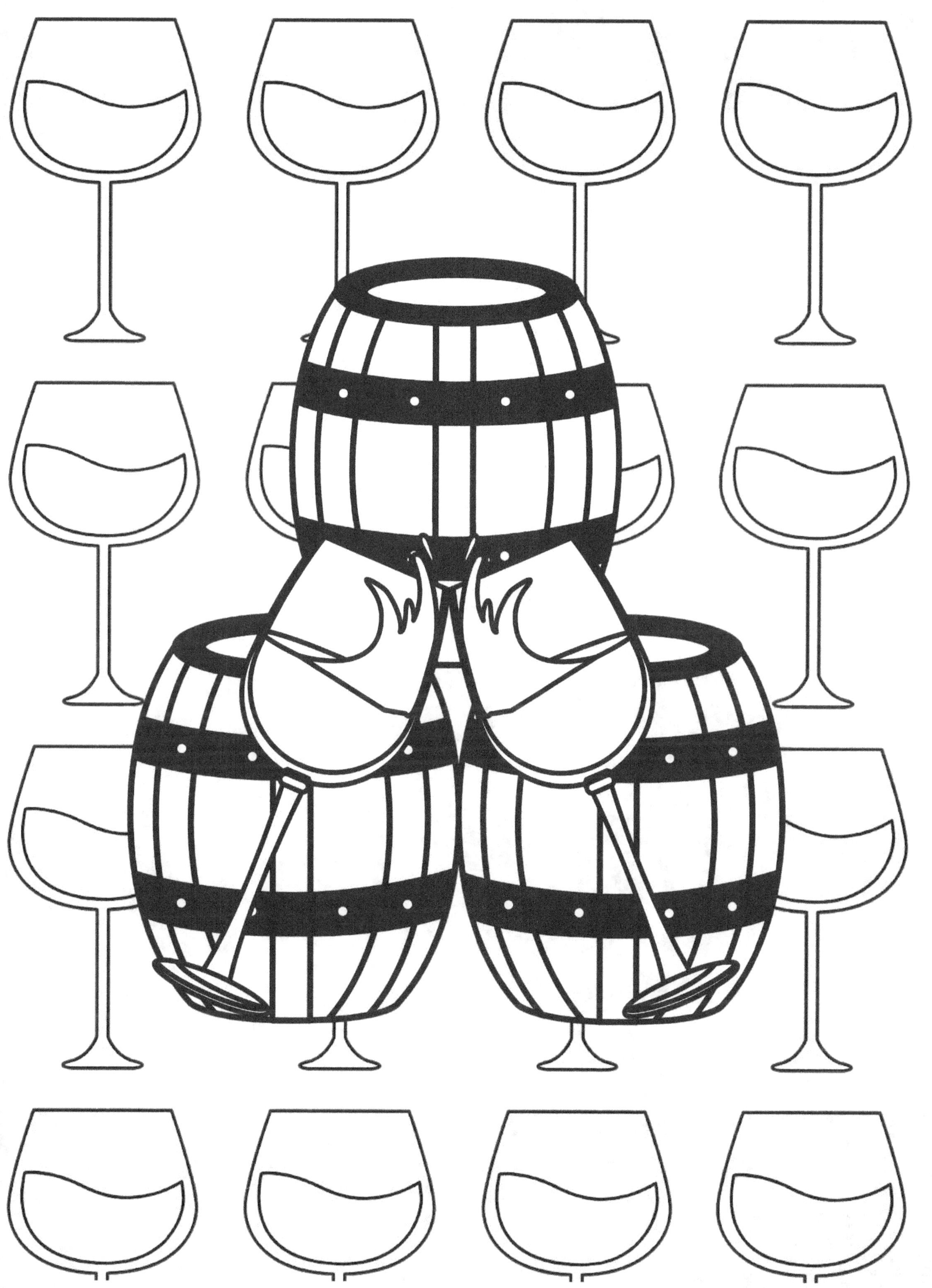